INVEST IN LIVING

ALL ABOUT HERBS

INVEST IN LIVING

ALL ABOUT HERBS

by

MAGGIE ANGELOGLOU

EP Publishing Limited
1977

About the Author

Maggie Angeloglou is a journalist, cook and novelist whose interest in the cultivation and use of herbs has developed over the years. She has established herb gardens for her own use under many varying conditions, and is fully aware of the problems encountered by herb-lovers who have very little space to spare—perhaps only a town balcony or even a windowsill.

At present she runs a restaurant in Northampton, where she uses home-grown herbs in cooking.

The author and publishers gratefully acknowledge the following for supplying photographs: Heather Angel (cover, top left), Marshall Cavendish Ltd/Photos: Steve Bicknell (cover, top right and bottom), Mary Evans Picture Library (p. 8), Harry Smith Horticultural Photographic Collection (pp. 10, 18, 27, 34, 39, 41, 47).

ISBN 0 7158 0480 4

Published 1977 by EP Publishing Ltd, East Ardsley, Wakefield, West Yorkshire WF3 2JN

Printed and bound in Great Britain by Butler & Tanner Ltd, Frome and London

Contents

5

1 ❧ The History of Herbs

Only a few years ago herbs were thought to be 'foreign' and exotic, almost the sole British concession to them being sage and onion stuffing; but as an interest in cooking spread, and as more and more aspiring cooks travelled abroad, herbs became fashionable. Belatedly so and sometimes sadly, because too often a housewife will buy an array of matching jars, each packed with dried herbs, place it on a warm shelf near the cooker—and then forget about most of the contents. The herbs are almost always wasted, not only because it isn't a good idea to keep dried herbs too long, but also because it is only by habitual use of any new flavour that you grow to appreciate it. Most cooks who use herbs to any extent find that custom encourages more and more experiments, until the palate demands herbs and flavouring in all kinds of food. A garlic enthusiast will reject some dishes which should have, but are lacking, its unique taste because they will 'be all wrong'; similarly, an appreciative eater who knows that a casserole needs thyme, or that a roast chicken demands tarragon, will feel cheated if there's no trace of the flavour in the dish.

Yes, using herbs does make one dissatisfied with ninety per cent of the food found in cafés or in tins, but what pleasure to define the herbs used in an unfamiliar dish, and how delightful to find a new flavour! It all sounds perhaps a bit snobbish, a little like recognising the year of a vintage wine by taste, but appreciating herbs, growing and using them is one of the cheapest pleasures of the gourmet world. You can buy a new sensation for the price of a packet of seeds. With luck and generous friends a new herb can cost nothing at all. Read on, then, and find out how to grow herbs and how to use them.

What are herbs? 'Aha,' you will say, 'those thingummies, well, plants of course', and then perhaps 'aromatic plants'. And it is in fact just those plants I am writing about, not spices which are brought from abroad and often dried and powdered. They have their own delights, but there are subtle differences between spices and herbs. The former are the real exotica; they represented the magnificent East to Western Europe. The trade routes of the medieval world were dependent on the spices which were so necessary when rancid meat had to be disguised by new flavours. Cities and civilisations were founded on the routes and methods by which pepper, cloves, ginger and cinnamon reached Western Europe. Spices were the powdered gold-dust of the Middle Ages—and herbs were poor relations.

In those days, when every man had some sort of garden, herbs were grown like weeds. Often they were undefined; any green stuff could be, and was, called a herb. A 'sallet of herbs' would include lettuce as well as burnet, lovage and parsley. These plants usually sauntered into

An illustration from the *Greta Herbal*. Some of the earliest printed books were herbals, which were about as necessary as a bible in the days when herbs provided medicines as well as flavours

the gardens from a neighbouring hillside or a bog. They were treated shamefully, one suspects, with no Baby Bio or potting compost to spur them on, but then most cooks wanted no more than a green plant which would grow in any corner and add a bit of flavour to stale meat or fish.

The process of discovering and classifying herbs must have caused a number of stomach upsets and even deaths, but by the later Middle Ages some sorting out had been done, and herbs had been separately identified. Many herbs which grow in British gardens originally grew wild in this country; there are a few outsiders, such as the curry plant, coriander and sage, which have been introduced and which flourish here, but not very many, and it is chastening to consider that all those 'unusual' imported European herbs such as oregano, chervil or sorrel, which now are considered innovations in the British diet, were commonplace in Elizabethan herb gardens.

Herbs were not only grown as flavourings, but were just as important for their medicinal values, and are still used in many ointments and medicines today. Readers of old herbals will be surprised by how often one plant was considered a cure-all for many ailments; perhaps the most useful was garlic, which could be taken as a cough cure, rubbed onto the body to alleviate rheumatism, and also made a passable glue!

The heyday of herbs in this country was probably the late sixteenth and seventeenth centuries, which was also the period when the first cookery books were written and when the country house could be a little kingdom on its own. Cut off from large cities by impassable roads and uncomfortable travelling conditions, the housewife kept a brew-house and still-room, and was doctor and cook to a large household. These were the women who bought the early cookery books and herbals, and it is their recipes which have been compiled to give us some insight into household conditions of their times. It was not only those unfortunate hysterics called witches who made marigold tea and bittersweet face lotions; they were part of the stock-in-trade of every lady.

In the eighteenth century many of the old habits died out—London was more accessible and more fashionable, and with an annual three months' absence from her estate when she stayed in town, the house-wife could not be bothered to make up jars and boxes of medicines and ointments. Herb-growing fell into abeyance except in more remote or old-fashioned families. The Victorian mode of life almost put paid to it altogether, for patent medicines could claim to cure everything for a shilling a bottle, so why spend hours and sometimes days filtering and pounding dried herbs? Besides, the great ladies no longer learned to cook; it would have been considered *outré* and vulgar if they exhibited a down-to-earth interest in ingredients when French chefs miraculously produced their grand concoctions. The simple fresh flavours were not appreciated—only the most expensive ingredients were used in fashionable houses, and so herbs came to be considered fuddy-duddy and then eccentric, both for medicinal use and for flavouring.

Ironically, it took a renewed interest in foreign food to permit an appreciation of home-grown herbs. Many women who were coaxed by Elizabeth David and her writing colleagues in the late 1940s into an understanding of French food found that the most elusive ingredients were fresh herbs, and since these were indispensable for sorrel sauce or *omelettes fines herbes*, they decided to grow their own. Many gardens had always had a little patch containing parsley, sage and mint; to these were added a variety of plants, many useful, some downright useless, but all emphasising the interest which many housewives developed in herbs after the Second World War, not only for cooking, but also for their charm and ornamental properties.

Herbals

It is difficult to tell where cookery books, medical manuals and herbals merged together, they were so similar. In time, however, the herbal became associated with home remedies, and although herbs were still featured in cookery books they were gradually phased into medical matters and away from the kitchen. Home medical treatments are always suspect and nobody should expect that herbs could effect the cures which would be made by a doctor using modern drugs. At their best, herbal medicines can alleviate some pains and will give you refreshing tisanes or infused teas; at their worst, when used as alternatives to real medicines, they might actually be dangerous.

Everyman His Own Doctor was the title of a tome which could be found in many homes in the country, and *The English Physician* was another book which seems to have been in print with annotations for almost a hundred years. Probably the most famous herbal published in England was Gerard's imposing *Historie of Plants*. He was not concerned only with herbs—any plant came into the scope of those books loosely termed herbals and Gerard's work contains an astonishing amount of information on each plant.

The Herb Garden

Great houses always had a patch for herbs, but perhaps one of the most potent influences in gardening has been the herb garden established at Sissinghurst Castle by Vita Sackville-West. In this small area

The herb garden at Sissinghurst. The formal 'Tudor' design is practical as well as ornamental: the paving stones reflect heat and keep the herbs separate yet easily accessible for cutting

she developed so many different types of herbs and gave them such a new vitality that many gardeners imitated her ideas and realised that, just as her 'all white' garden could be repeated with credit, so her all-herb garden could be an ideal way to combine subtle colours (herbs have differing foliage) with aromatic smells by using unusual plants. The herb garden became a conversation piece.

It is still one of the best ways to utilise a small town garden; since many herbs can be packed into a small area, and as they look their best in between brick paths or spilling out of troughs and terraces, they form almost the best type of garden for those who are restricted by room and even restricted in pocket. Most good herbs are perennials so there is no need to spend much money after the first year; they fulfil several demands, not only for flavourings but also as foliage for cut flowers, and their 'green dream' patterns fill a border with delightful spreading shapes from early spring until the winter. A herb garden enchants visitors, not only for its character but also because a slow walk about even the smallest area gives us such a variety of sensations—a leaf to rub, a flower to smell, and always a tiny sprig to taste. Beware though, the taste of a raw herb may be no real indication of how it will be when the chemistry of cooking has worked on it.

There are instructions for making herb gardens in Chapter 3, so here I will only make one point: if you are short of room and wish to have an unusual and useful garden, you should forget lawns, shrubs and herbaceous borders—a herb garden will give you more pleasure than any of them.

2 ～ Herbs in a Small Space

You might imagine a herb garden as a secluded corner of a much larger kitchen garden, but perhaps beguilingly near the kitchen itself, so that you could run out and crop a few handfuls of sage or thyme for the pot. But that notion of a herb garden has diminished since the days of head gardeners and half-acre lawns—just as the patio has replaced the eighty-foot terrace, so herb gardening has been cut to a minimum of space. It can even exist in a row of pots on a town window ledge.

Note: For a detailed description of the cultivation and uses of each herb, see Chapter 4.

Balcony Herbs

Unfortunately, shrubby herbs are not practical for most town kitchens. It is true that an outsize pot can accommodate a rosemary or sage plant, but the root run would be minimal and few shrubs can exist happily in a kitchen atmosphere. However, they would grow very well in large pots on a balcony and if you have a tiny terrace it could be used advantageously. Rosemary needs protection from frosts and cold winds but is otherwise a very biddable balcony plant and its spiky dark green foliage, which is interesting in winter as well as summer, acts as a splendid foil to white petunias, pot marigolds and geraniums. Put it next to a bay tree, which is also unhappy in cold weather, but do remember that both rose-

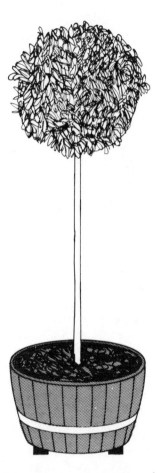

mary and bay must winter in a sheltered position. Straw round the roots and a glass roof over their heads are often good enough, but if you have a tiny concrete terrace nine floors up and facing north, forget shrub herbs in flower-pots; they would never last longer than one summer season and, while it is true they can be replaced, it would be a pity to waste them.

Parsley, chives and thyme are useful and suitable herbs to grow in pots on a windowsill

Windowsill Herbs

Annuals are easy to grow in pots, but though their foliage is decorative few are basic enough to be used more than a few times a year. If you do grow annuals, sow basil and dill—both have practical uses and basil, especially, can last well into autumn given the right conditions. Both take kindly to pot culture. Dill is a graceful plant, with soft 'maidenhair' leaves of deep green, but basil, one must face it, looks rather like chickweed, sprawling and round-leaved but with a bright green colour. In a kitchen it is nice to have herbs which have gratifying smells as well as looks, and dill is a good herb for emitting its fragrance when pinched.

Chervil is another useful annual from the culinary point of view, but unfortunately it has a very short season.

If space on your windowsill is limited, restrict your growing to a few herbs which will give you most practical value; as you will read in the next chapter, these are not always adaptable to pot culture, but an apple mint should thrive, and so will parsley. It's a good idea to have one plant which can be used in a salad, sprinkled over lettuce and cucumber to add an interesting extra flavour—lovage and burnet are very good for this. Chives are another possibility.

Thyme is one of the best subjects for pot culture, and you will find it useful to have two varieties so that one plant can be cut back and allowed to grow again. Tarragon might do better in a pot on a warm window ledge than it does in the garden. It can become very leggy and need a lot of staking, though, and it should be cut often or new shoots won't develop so easily from the base. Make sure you have French tarragon. It's expensive, so if you can collect it from a nursery pick the most bushy and wide-spreading plant and take a cutting as soon as possible so that it doesn't die back and leave you without a substitute.

Other candidates for the pot are caraway

and lemon balm, though neither of them is top priority for somebody who is short of space. Perhaps you might consider them for a larger container.

Herbs have the same basic needs as most pot plants; they need a sunlit position and if they are actually on your kitchen window-sill they will prefer fresh air to a fat-laden, steamy atmosphere. If your kitchen is poorly ventilated it might be kinder to grow your herbs in another part of the flat or house. Ideally a wide ledge and lots of glass suit them, so if you have a suitable hall or even a bathroom, preferably facing south, make that the site of your container-grown herb garden. However, a few herbs need such large pots that it could be better to invest in a window-box or two if you can.

If you wish to grow your plants from seed, follow the instructions given on p. 20. If you want to buy ready-grown plants, choose a reputable nursery or garden centre and pick the sturdiest-looking plants.

Plant your herbs in a compost such as John Innes No. 1, and use earthenware pots if possible. After an era of plastic, the once familiar terracotta flower-pots are on the market again. Not only do they look better, but they are porous and retain water so that plants can be left unwatered for a few days if you go away. Before planting the herb, put some drainage material in the base of the pot. Ideally this should be shards of a similar pot if you can find a broken one, but if this is impossible use largish stones, to ensure that the plant doesn't become waterlogged.

Fill the pot halfway with compost then insert the plant firmly, lightly splaying out the roots with your fingers. Dribble more compost round the plant until the pot is filled to within about 12 mm ($\frac{1}{2}$ in) of the rim, to allow space for watering. Firm down the compost around the main stem of the plant. If it came in a container you will see that there is a natural line of demarcation where the roots join the main stem, so aim to bring the compost just above the joint. Make sure that the plant is firm; a

Some herbs will need support from a stake

little pressure with your knuckles round the stem will be necessary, and you will be able to see for yourself if the plant is erect and stable. You might need to put a thin stake into the compost—many herbs will simply need something to lean against, a sort of wooden lamp-post, but bigger, leggier specimens might need a little raffia to hold them to the stake.

After planting, water freely. The compost should be sticky, rather like a good bread dough, so that it clings to the fingers but isn't swimmy with water. A little dry compost on the top is sometimes a good idea. Make sure you have a saucer or a dish for the pot to rest in. This is not an ornament but an essential part of pot culture, for many plants prefer being watered from the base and the dish will hold a residue if you go away and need to leave enough water for your plants.

Don't become too involved with watering; many plants of all kinds are drowned. Overwatering can lead to as much trouble

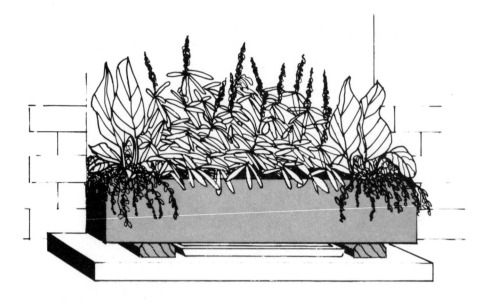

as underwatering. Don't make a timetable of your watering, but watch the plant instead. The weather and the growing habit will determine how much water a plant needs—in winter it will use very little for it will be resting. In the spring, when it is putting out new shoots, it will need more water and perhaps a little feeding mixture. In summer the compost will dry rapidly and the plant might need watering once a day, especially if it is on a warm windowsill where the glass increases the power of the sun. On very hot days it might be as well to remove the plant from the window or draw a blind or a net curtain to screen the foliage from the sunlight. This will only happen rarely, but look out for those torrid days when leaves wilt and turn yellow.

If you have a small watering can, fill it with water in the morning and leave it near the pots to adapt to the temperature around it. It may even end up being luke-warm, but this is the temperature the plant needs after a hot day, when cold water would frizzle the roots and foliage. Water as late in the evening as possible after a hot day so that the plant, its pot and the compost have all cooled down and can receive water gladly.

Window-boxes

At one time few window-boxes contained more adventurous plants than geraniums and lobelia, but with renewed interest in self-sufficiency window-boxes are used for melons, tomatoes, aubergines and beans. And of course they give herbs a bigger root run and more chance of expansion.

Before you plant a window-box, consider your main objective. If you want it to be decorative, perhaps spanning the most important façade of the house, you can use herbs, but only in a repetitive way. If you try to plant all the varieties in which you are interested, you will have more pleasure in cooking, but your window-box will look higgledy-piggledy, with differing types of foliage and heights along it. Ornamental window-boxes are usually unprofitable to the cook, who will appreciate that six rosemary plants will give her too much rosemary and there will be no room left for oregano, thyme or parsley.

An ambitious gardener in a flat could have two boxes, one for show and one for use. However, there is no need to banish herbs altogether from a decorative window-box. It could contain a central swathe of rosemary or the traditional English dwarf lavender, which could be fronted with shorter pot marigolds, and the edges of the box could be planted with a creeping rockery thyme which would flow down the sides of the box, with trailing nasturtiums. If the window-box is in a very sheltered position or screened by glass, the central plants could be the oak-leafed *geranium quercifolium*, a plant which grows very strongly and has an attractive scented leaf, and is often seen in the windows of Cypriot, Greek and Turkish restaurants. Its leaves are traditionally used to flavour stews in the Mediterranean countries and they have a delightful fragrance which is apparent when the leaves are rubbed. The flowers are insignificant but the foliage is luxuriant, and the plant is easily propagated by cuttings.

Bay trees, or bushes, are also a good choice for the tall plant in a window-box; cutting back will keep them a reasonable size and ensure that the roots don't become too demanding for the depth of the box. However, their plain laurel-leaved foliage is very tender, and also very dull; a window-box of bay would need bright flowers to set it off.

There is no reason why the flowers surrounding a herb should not be chosen for their uses, too. An enthusiastic pot-pourri maker, for instance, might wish to edge a box of rosemary or lavender with old-fashioned pinks like Mrs Sinkins, the common white garden pink which can be dried and used in sachets and herb pillows. Other scented plants for pot-pourri include roses, lemon verbena, basil and tarragon. Violet heads and white jasmine might not come from a window-box but could be grown in pots on a London balcony.

Plants which are not in any way herbal but which consort well with herbs in window-boxes include mignonette, snapdragons (antirrhinums), petunias and campanulas. Ivy-leafed trailing geraniums can be used to screen the sides of a window-box. Modern versions of the window-box are often fairly unsightly, and fortunately there are plenty of plants which can overflow the container and not only hide its walls but also give an illusion of a spilling cornucopia which can be all the more attractive when seen from the regimentation of a busy city street.

If you are fortunate enough to have another window-box in the kitchen, it could be used for the more utilitarian purpose of growing all those plants which are also suitable for pots—parsley, mint, chives, thyme and basil—plus some of the larger plants which cannot be fitted into pots, such as rosemary or sage. There are a few plants which are not basic herbs but which might be added if you aren't short of space, and which can be very useful in the summer. One is chervil, which is like a much more delicate parsley. Another is borage, which could be grown simply because it attracts bees; the perpetual humming about its pretty blue flowers could bring summer very pleasantly into a town flat, but borage is also most useful as a flavouring for summer drinks. Both chervil and borage are annuals and can be grown easily from seed.

You might also grow marjoram; the difference between the varieties is explained on p. 38, and the most suitable one to choose is probably pot marjoram, which can be treated as a perennial and is propagated most successfully by division. Another candidate for the window-box is savory, which again has subdivisions. Summer savory is an annual very like thyme, so the winter variety is a better choice for the window-box, although its flavour is supposedly inferior; it is a perennial and quite tough, and can usually produce a few leaves during the colder months, so that if your thyme dies back completely, winter savory can be used as a substitute.

If you intend to grow herbs in a window-box, a good investment is a sprayer of the atomiser type, which throws out a very fine mist and is invaluable for keeping foliage clean and free of dust.

3 ～ Location and Propagation

Most herbs benefit from sunshine because they are imported plants which are used to warmer climates; for instance, thyme comes from the Mediterranean, verbena from Chile, and oregano from Italy. However, many plants have taken to our weather well enough to survive the winters, although a sheltered position is best for a herb garden, as many of the plants cannot withstand cold winds even if they are not affected by frost.

Don't despair if the herb garden becomes barren in winter; probably eighty per cent of herbs die back in cold weather and it is a good idea to put peat, dried bracken or straw over the ground during the colder months so that the plants are protected underground and will come through again in March. It is very helpful to label the position of each plant—even if this seems unnecessary in summer, it will be useful in the winter.

A large herb garden should be complemented by some winter storage space such as a shed, a cool greenhouse or even a spare bedroom where plants which need shelter can be kept in pots with very little water and a modicum of light until the spring.

Many herbs benefit from well-manured earth, and if you are establishing a new herb garden dig some well-decayed manure or compost well into the soil before you begin. Dried blood and bone are good additions too. Several of the herbs, such as comfrey and horseradish, have very deep roots. It is true that plants from the Mediterranean and the mountains can flourish in dry stony ground, but a little manure helps most of them to become established.

If you are sowing seed directly into the herb border, the soil should be quite friable and well worked, even if you have to sieve it to achieve the right degree of fine tilth; however, if you grow from seed in boxes and plant established plants or cuttings it is less important to have well-worked soil— many herbs quite like stony, restricted ground and, given the right temperature, will survive almost anywhere. Usually, they do not need as much cosseting as flowers and vegetables.

Unfortunately this sturdiness can have disadvantages as a few herbs will rampage all over the rest of the garden: mint, horseradish and, to some degree, comfrey, should all be restrained in some way, in sunken pots, securely bricked plots, tin cans of some sort, or even in old chimney-pots which can be pushed down into the earth. If you do not confine them, you will have to keep an eye on the growth of these herbs and check them if necessary—a little rain and they will take over the plot.

Although the ideal situation is a sheltered border, facing south, preferably with a slope, most of us cannot be so selective when we choose a site for a herb garden, for in spite of all these requirements the

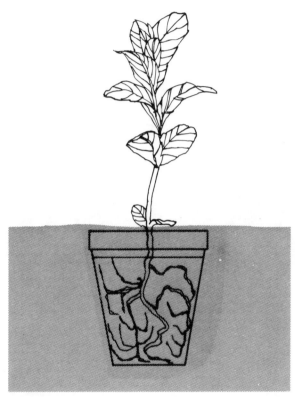

Stop vigorous herbs like mint from taking over the herb garden by growing them in a pot which is sunk in the earth

most important specification is that the herb garden must be near the kitchen; if this is impossible, for instance if there is a large yard at the back of the house, or a cold dank area basement, think in terms of two herb centres. Plant a window-box or pots for immediate use in the kitchen, and grow mint, parsley, thyme and tarragon in them; and establish a place for herbs in a more distant vegetable garden where savory, sorrel and other more demanding herbs can be grown and picked twice a week to be kept in a jar of water on the kitchen windowsill. Most cooks will journey to a vegetable garden several times a week at least, in order to pick vegetables, and greater quantities of herbs can be picked at the same time. Many herbs prefer the company of other plants, so a vegetable plot can be very suitable. Moreover, some herbs deter slugs, which can be a most useful bonus; indeed, it might be worth using a fringe of pennyroyal to fence off fleshy-leaved plants in the garden which may be particularly attractive to slugs and caterpillars.

Steady pruning keeps lavender healthy and ornamental

Herb gardens are often set into brick walks or paved edgings. This has a more practical than decorative use, for the bricks reflect the sun and any herb garden will be happier if it is set against a brick wall or has some low brick walls near it.

If the garden is windswept, erect artificial windbreaks. In time these can be supplemented with close-cropped lavender bushes (not rosemary, which is tender) or box hedges, but initially you might use wattle hurdles which will screen effectively until a suitable hedge has grown. Make sure, however, that your windbreak does not take away sunlight from the herbs, for sun is absolutely necessary for many plants in the border. If wattle hurdles cast too much shade on the herbs, erect a screen of widely spaced mesh or trellis and trail over it a quick-growing climbing plant which will not impinge on the herbs. Clematis montana, honeysuckle or Russian vine are good choices, providing it is not too cold for them. If you are in a particularly chilly windblown area, try bushes of sea buckthorn or broom, keeping them clipped back so that they do not dwarf the herbs. Both are ornamental as well as useful windbreaks.

A hedge is only feasible if you have

enough rich soil to permit the growth of all the plants; privet, for instance, will take all the goodness away from the herb border and all the sunlight as well.

If you have a town garden or a patio, consider raised beds such as troughs which could be filled with a mixture of good topsoil and compost to make a sheltered, easily run herb garden. A raised garden is a blessing for weeding, cropping and drainage, provided that those herbs which need moisture are not neglected. A depth of 1 m (3 ft 3 in) would be adequate for most herbs—obviously you would have to avoid the more deep-growing varieties, but these are usually rampant and would not be suitable for a restricted area anyway. In making a raised garden, you can ensure that the best soil elements are combined in it—and don't forget to include plenty of worms!

If you have a large flat area to be covered by herbs, insert a few large stepping-stones as you form the garden. There is nothing more exasperating than attempting to gather a herb which is beyond reach, and as the herbs flourish and grow closer together you will be unable to pick the ones at the back without treading on some of the plants.

If you have a large potential herb garden and enough time and money, design an Elizabethan formal garden with brick walks in the shape of a star or cartwheel so that you can walk about between the herbs; the pleasure will be increased by the aroma of herbs brushed by your clothing as you pass. A garden seat is an added delight in a herb garden. The simple teak type suits the monochromatic colours of the herbs, but you might like to try and copy an ornament in a famous herb garden, which is a wide stone sink planted with camomile. This herb can be grown as a lawn and could cover any grass area in a herb garden as it smells sweetly when trodden on; however, it must be clipped with shears, not mown.

If you grow herbs all over your garden, you may wish to interplant other flowers to complement them and to keep the area lively during those months when herbs die back. Roses have a particular affinity with herbs, and evergreens are also a good idea, providing they are kept short and don't take away too much sunlight or good soil. Otherwise, plunge heavily for scented plants: pinks, mignonette, sweet william, dianthus, violas, and the edging plants common to rockeries, such as campanulas and aubretias.

Flowers which consort well with herbs are akin to them; marigolds, nasturtiums and violets can be used in the kitchen. Consider also the possibility of sprinkling Alpine strawberry plants among the herbs—the fringed leaf is very attractive, the white and gold flowers could ornament any flower border, and the tiny sweet fruit can be gathered all summer. While the herb garden is still dank and dull, in early spring, it is a good plan to have an array of bulbs to make a splash of colour. Small narcissi, snowdrops or scilla take up very little room and if they are grown in clumps they can be left undisturbed all year.

Once planted, herbs need very little care. Often they need less water than herbaceous plants, but do not deprive them altogether. They will quickly form a mass of blue-greenery and their rampant habits will keep down weeds. Few insects care for herbs, but the most susceptible are those with fleshy leaves such as horseradish. A discreet planting of thyme and pennyroyal will screen the herbs from invaders. Garlic, chives, rue and lavender also deter pests and in time these should make a barrier. It helps to crush a few leaves daily so that the aromatic oils will pervade the air and keep slugs away. Derris dust and pyrethrum powder can be used as insecticides. Commercial sprays are not always suitable—remember that you may soon be eating the leaves you have sprayed!

Growing From Seed

If you wish to grow your plants from seed, follow the instructions on the seed-packets regarding the time to sow, depth of the seeds, etc. You would be wise to start off all your seeds in trays or pots indoors or in a greenhouse, though it is not essential. If you are growing for a window-sill herb garden, sow straight into the pots, in ordinary compost, and there will be no need to transplant. Sow more seeds than you will need plants and weed out all but two or three of the sturdiest seedlings later.

If you are going to transplant the seedlings, it is best to start them off in a proprietary seed compost. Fill your container to within 12 mm ($\frac{1}{2}$ in) of the top and wet the compost thoroughly. Sow the seeds thinly and cover with a compost layer of the prescribed depth; very small seeds may not need covering at all.

If you are using a pot, place a polythene bag over the top and secure it with a rubber band; if you are starting your seeds off in a seed-tray, cover it with polythene or glass. Place the container in a shady place. Keep the compost moist (a small watering can with a fine rose is useful, as you don't want to wash away the seeds), and as soon as the seedlings show through, remove the polythene or glass and move the container into full light (e.g. on a windowsill if you are growing seeds indoors).

Covering a pot containing newly sown seeds with polythene will help to conserve the moisture

The right time to transplant—when the seedlings have four leaves

Wait until the seedlings have four leaves; if they are destined for pots indoors, now is the time to transplant them. If they are for the garden, put the container in the open air, with shelter, preferably on a raised bench or a shelf of bricks. About ten days later the seedlings will have hardened off and can be planted out. Make sure the earth is well raked and water the soil about an hour before you plant out if it has not recently rained. The ground should be moist and finely textured. Plant in the early evening, when the earth is cooling but not too cold, and water the area round the plant after planting, taking care not to dampen the foliage. Your seed-packet should tell you the distance at which to space the plants. Make sure your new herb is well labelled. It's a good idea to plant more seedlings than you will ultimately need, partly to allow for loss of plants but also because you will have so many plants from a tiny packet that it seems wasteful not to use them. If you have far too many seedlings, place some in tiny pots and keep them for indoor cultivation, or give them away.

Cuttings

If you are allowing your herbs to flower, for either ornamental or seed purpose, take cuttings after they have flowered. If you are avoiding a flowering period, take cuttings

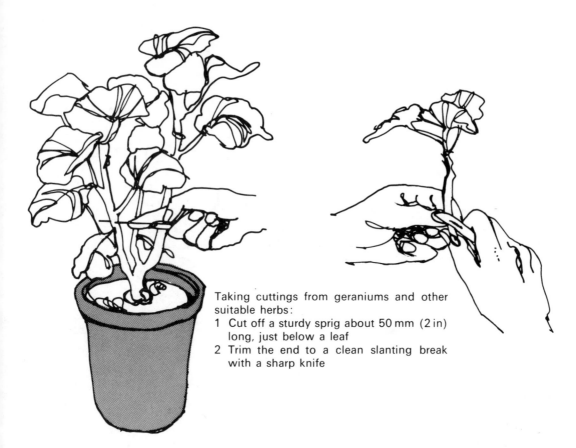

Taking cuttings from geraniums and other suitable herbs:
1 Cut off a sturdy sprig about 50 mm (2 in) long, just below a leaf
2 Trim the end to a clean slanting break with a sharp knife

when the new sprigs which grew in spring have had time to harden—often the late summer is best. Your local gardening centre will probably have bags of suitable compost made up, and I find it better to rely on these than to make up my own compost. The cost is higher but you will have less worry and work. If you do wish to make your own compost, mix equal quantities of sand, garden loam and peat and add a sprinkling of lime.

Fill the pots to within 12 mm ($\frac{1}{2}$ in) of the rim with the compost mixture, and take your cuttings by clipping off a sprig about 50 mm (2 in) long, just below a leaf on the main stem. Make sure that you have a slanting clean break, using a razor blade or Stanley knife if possible, though the cutting can be trimmed to a clean break afterwards. If you can get a cutting with the beginnings of a new growth to one side, especially with a

geranium, so much the better; a little V-shaped sprig will be stronger and grow better.

Insert the end of the cutting in rooting powder, which contains chemicals to encourage growth. Place the cuttings round the edge of the pot; the compost will be damp, but to ensure that the cuttings keep fresh and healthy, spray them with an atomiser. The latter has already been mentioned as being useful for window-boxes, and it will also prove a good friend to your cuttings, keeping the leaves and soil clean and moist. A cutting will keep alive for a long time in these conditions without necessarily forming a root, so be patient. The best test of whether a cutting has 'taken' is to see if new leaves form, but this may take quite some time. Only transplant those cuttings which have new leaves.

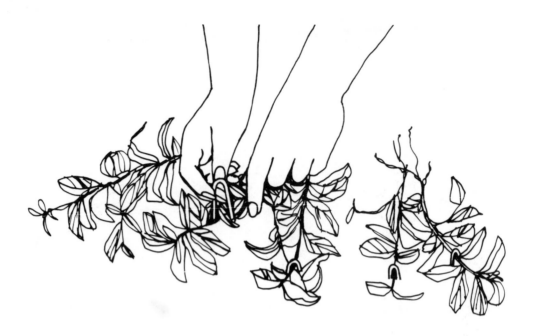

Verbena, like some other herbs, is easy to propagate by layering. Simply peg shoots down to the soil with a hairpin

Layering

Many plants propagate themselves by layering. A prostrate branch will send suckers down into suitable soil; ivy is the most common wild example, and pinks are easily propagated in this way in the garden. Woody supple plants like rosemary, thymes, mints, marjoram, verbena and balm can be rooted this way. Geraniums can also be layered, but as their stems are less flexible they can be accidentally snapped off. Choose a whippy, healthy stem, bend it so that the stem is on the ground, moisten the earth under the stem and clip the stem to the soil with an old-fashioned U-shaped hairpin. A clothes peg would do if necessary, but a hairpin is better as it is tenacious and yet lightweight. Some gardeners slit the underneath of the stem to encourage root formation, but you have to be very adept to open the skin and not the centre of the stem—too deep a wound could snip off the stem. It's better to allow the plant to

send out its own roots, as it will after a few weeks. Six weeks will usually see the new plant thriving, and the bent stem can be cut from the parent plant. The chief requirement of this method of propagation is enough spare earth; apart from that it is very simple, and often the new plant is larger than that formed from a cutting and more resilient as it has lived outdoors all the time and has had no removal problems.

4 ∽ The Border∽30 Herbs

You may establish a more than adequate herb garden with far less than thirty herbs, but a border measuring 3.7 m × 1.8 m (approx. 12 ft × 6 ft) can accommodate thirty varieties quite easily. At first they may look rather sparse, and it will be tempting to arrange the heights according to the sizes of the plants which are bought from the nursery. However, the plan on p. 24 shows the herbs arranged according to *potential* size, and if it seems lunatic to place a minute lovage plant at the back of the border, where the sorrel in front will at first tower over it, remember that the lovage may eventually grow up to 2 m (over 6 ft) tall, while the sorrel may stop at about 750 mm (2 ft 6 in). This is a plan for the established border, not for the first season. If you are courageous and are worried by the fact that the arrangement looks peculiar in the first year, arrange the plants according to their current sizes, bearing in mind that they may all have to be transplanted in the second spring. The annuals are the easiest plants of all; they will not have to be organised beyond the first year.

This imaginary border could be at the end of anybody's back garden, but from my own experience it is better for it to be at the beginning. The most successful herb garden I have cultivated was in a minute London back garden which could be more accurately described as a patio. There was a narrow concrete path between the house and the garden, which was initially a small patch of grass surrounded by narrow flower borders. I dug up the lawn, which sloped downhill to the house, and made a raised border between the path and the main garden. Being tiered, it had many advantages for the gardener and the cook; as it sloped upwards every plant could be seen and identified immediately. Weeding and plucking could be done with very little bending or kneeling, and the most commonly used plants could be grabbed almost by leaning out of the kitchen door!

The plan assumes a wall at the back of the border. This is not essential, but some sort of wall or fence is useful to provide shelter. Every garden has some shade, often created by an elderly deciduous tree. If you are starting from scratch, plant your own shade tree to complement the herb garden by being both useful and ornamental. A cherry tree, a John Downie crab apple, a Victoria plum or a pear tree are all decorative and useful, and the bush varieties don't take up much space. If you like the appearance of an established tree, buy a mulberry which looks gnarled in its first season. The mulberries, which will fall all over the herbs, will act as compost. You can eat them too. If you want a tree that will not take up too much room but will look attractive with the herb garden, you might plant a rowan (or mountain ash), which has a graceful leaf allowing dappled shadows to fall, as

23

30 Herbs in a Border

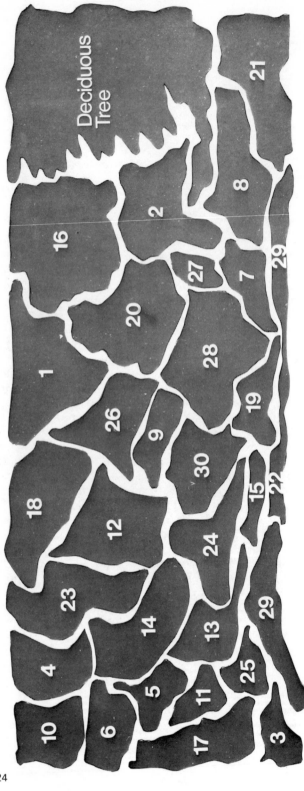

Deciduous Tree

1. **Angelica.** 1.8–2.5 m (6–8 ft) high, 900 mm (3 ft) wide. Biennial. Moist position, partial shade. (Gives partial shade to mint.)
2. **Balm or Lemon Balm.** 600–900 mm (2–3 ft). Perennial. Moist soil, partial shade.
3. **Basil.** 300–600 mm (1–2 ft). Annual. Sunny position.
4. **Bay Tree.** Perennial. Needs sun, water and shelter.
5. **Bergamot.** 900 mm (3 ft). Perennial. Needs mulch.
6. **Borage.** 600–900 mm (2–3 ft). Annual. Sunny position.
7. **Burnet.** 300–600 mm (1–2 ft). Perennial.
8. **Chervil.** 300–600 mm (1–2 ft). Annual. Needs semi-shade. Short-lived.
9. **Chives.** 300 mm (1 ft). Perennial.
10. **Comfrey.** 0.9–1.2 m (3–4 ft). Perennial. Deep soil. Makes compost.
11. **Dill.** 600 mm (2 ft). Annual.
12. **Fennel.** 1.2 m (4 ft). Perennial (or Annual). Sunny position.
13. **Scented-leaved Geranium.** 600 mm (2 ft). Perennial. Sun and shelter.
14. **Horseradish.** 850 mm (2½ ft). Perennial. Grow in container or eliminate side growth. Deep rich soil, sun and moisture.
15. **Hyssop.** 450 mm (1½ ft). Perennial. Sunny position.
16. **Juniper Communis.** 1.2 m (4 ft). Perennial. Gives partial shade when mature.
17. **Lavender.** 0.6–1.2 m (2–4 ft). Perennial. Sunny position.
18. **Lovage.** Up to 2 m (6 ft) but starts small. Perennial. Sun or partial shade. Rich moist soil.
19. **Marjoram.** 300–450 mm (1–1½ ft). Perennial or Annual. Sunny position.
20. **Mint.** 600–900 mm (2–3 ft). Perennial. Grow in container. Moist position, semi-shade or sun.
21. **Parsley.** 300–450 mm (1–1½ ft). Biennial. Deep, rich soil, shade.
22. **Pennyroyal.** Under 300 mm (1 ft). Perennial. Edging plant.
23. **Rosemary.** 0.9–1.8 m (3–6 ft). Perennial. Light soil, sun and shelter.
24. **Sage.** 900 mm (3 ft). Perennial. Sun, dry soil.
25. **Savory.** Annual or Perennial.
26. **French Sorrel.** 750 mm (2½ ft) or more. Perennial. Sun or semi-shade.
27. **Sweet Cicely.** 900 mm (3 ft). Perennial.
28. **Tarragon.** 750 mm (2½ ft) high, 1.2 m (4 ft) wide when grown. Perennial. Must have sun. Needs protection in winter.
29. **Lemon Thyme.** 150 mm (6 in). Sun. Edging plant.
30. **Lemon Verbena.** 450–600 mm (1½–2 ft). Perennial.

well as red berries which can be made into rowan jelly to eat with cold meat and game.

Another possibility, which is purely decorative, is the silver-leafed willow pear, which is an ornamental tree of pendulous habit with a distinctive willow appearance and long, narrow, silvery leaves which look like grey suède. This is the same colour as many herbs so that it will 'act out' the theme repeated below it in sage, southernwood, curry plants, rue or lavender. If your garden is a suntrap and if you are short of deep rich earth, and also if your herb garden backs onto a wall, you could plant a fig tree. Figs prefer a restricted root run and so they would provide shelter and shade for the herbs beneath them without sucking too much goodness from the soil.

Another shademaker in a suntrap garden is a vine, which could be made to clamber over a pergola topped by grass matting, providing shade for some herbs, and incidentally a bower for the gardener.

At the other end of the border is a bay tree, which also creates problems, needing both shelter and sun. Pressed near to the wall it should have both, but on the left-hand side of the border there should be a firm windbreak which will screen the bay but not shut the sun from the other plants. A low wattle hurdle covered with clematis montana is a good screen; this clematis, which is the small-flowered type which grows rapidly, will thicken on the hurdles to form a dense screen. Providing it is kept to less than 1.2 m (4 ft) high, it will act as a blanket for the bay, and if it is cut back at the front the sun should penetrate to plants nearer the front of the border. Lavender, kept well trimmed, will cosset the front and side of the bay; these sturdy bushes are very tough windbreaks.

You will notice that several of the plants shown seem to have no use in today's kitchen, and it is true that many herb gardeners include them for merely sentimental reasons, although it is tempting to find a purpose for them by hunting for old recipes. However, angelica, bergamot, hyssop, pennyroyal, comfrey and verbena do have some purpose in this herb border, if only to break up the design with a new texture or to add a spot of colour in the general greenery. Do not dismiss your herb garden as dull in the first year; when they are tiny insignificant plants many herbs look ready for the rubbish heap. It needs a good growing year for them to burgeon, and when they do you will be well rewarded for your patience. Most herbs have delightful growing habits and shapes, and will spread with much more enthusiasm than many herbaceous plants, developing a type of controlled wilderness in which spires of sorrel or umbrellas of fennel stand up from a delightful spread of thick luxuriant foliage.

There follows information on 30 of the most useful herbs, including cultural tips and an outline of the basic uses of each herb in the kitchen. Specific recipes are given in Chapter 6.

1. Angelica

This is an umbelliferous plant with fleshy stems and well-shaped divided leaves. In this herb garden it will form a backcloth, as fortunately it likes partial shade and a rich moist soil. Make sure that the seeds are absolutely fresh when they are sown. If you have a friend with a plant, you can ensure that the seeds are ripe and are not past their germinating period. Seeds from seedsmen should have been sealed swiftly into their packets, so they should germinate successfully. Plant the seeds 25 mm (1 in) deep in very well dug soil for a deep root run. Established plants may well develop seedlings in the second year from dropped seed, but if you wish, this biennial can be made perennial by pruning back before the flowers set in.

Angelica can be candied for use in cakes and tarts, and traditionally it accompanied ginger flavouring to reduce the sharpness. A recipe for crystallised angelica can be found on p. 54. Angelica leaves have a charming scent and will perfume a room if they are used for flower decoration. As they are not long-lasting, they are only suitable for dinner table posies.

2. Balm

Also known as melissa or lemon balm, this springtime herb should not be used too late in the season, as the leaves lose their appealing lemon flavour. It grows in shady places where the soil is rich and moist, and has a rampant root run which might need to be checked. Cut the plant back in the autumn. In the summer its small white flowers are a great attraction for bees; traditionally fruit growers used to plant lemon balm round the trunks of fruit trees to encourage bees for pollination, and there is no reason why this charming and practical idea shouldn't be used today.

As it is one of the mint family, balm develops many smaller plants off its roots, which can be used for propagation. If seed is saved from the flowers it should be soaked in water overnight before planting, as it has a hard coating which should be softened to aid germination. In spite of enjoying partial shade, the leaves can blanch in too much shade, so don't bury the plant under a tree but make sure some sunshine penetrates to it during part of the day.

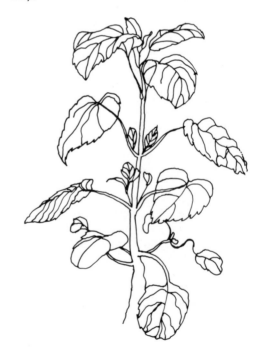

Angelica (seen in the foreground of this photograph) can be ornamental in a general flower border

Variegated balm is often offered to the gardener. This is more of a border plant with little culinary virtue, but its parti-coloured leaves look pretty and will bring the scent of balm into the house in flower arrangements. It needs to be protected from frost in winter.

Balm leaves retain their smell long after cutting, so it was one of the herbs used in a dried form to freshen rooms in Elizabethan times; because of this it is a favourite ingredient of pot pourri.

Balm is used mainly in stuffings and sauces for chicken and duck, but it can also be used for dressing fresh fruit salads, and for flavouring fruit cooked in red wine or syrup.

3. Basil

Basil is a popular herb, but unfortunately it is an annual. Its smell can be a bit off-putting initially, being slightly catty, but once you are used to it you will like its rather bitter scent, and the flavour is excellent.

There are two types of basil, the sweet and bush varieties. Bush basil is very short, about 150 mm (6 in) high, but sweet basil can grow to 600 mm (2 ft). Basil seeds germinate quickly and you will soon have a sturdy plant, but it will flourish better if the florets are pinched out regularly so that a wide, bushy shape develops. Although it is an annual, basil can be obtained in the winter by planting seeds in the middle of the summer and bringing the seedlings indoors in pots in autumn. Some gardeners in warm areas have been able to make their plants perennials by cutting them right back in the autumn, but you have to have a fairly frost-free sheltered growing area for this to succeed.

Basil cannot be dried easily, but the leaves will keep well for winter if they are layered with salt in a pot which is then closely covered. Another way to keep basil is in olive oil—you could flavour both the oil and your winter cookery by tying a bunch of basil and putting it into an oil-filled wide-mouthed glass jar with a screw-top. It makes a pretty kitchen decoration, too.

Basil is supposed to keep flies away and some Mediterranean restaurants keep pots of it on outdoor tables in the summer. Basil can be used in many dishes, especially those from Italy, but its real affinity is with tomatoes, and fresh sliced tomatoes dotted with basil leaves make one of the best salads imaginable.

4. Bay

The Roman laurel, used for crowning poets, bay is one of the most commonly used herbs, not only as part of a *bouquet garni* but also on its own, in casseroles, milk puddings and fish dishes. One of its attributes is that it can be lifted completely out of a dish, leaving its flavour behind. Although young bay trees can be delicate and should be grown in a sheltered place, a large mature tree seems to acquire enough strength to stay outside all winter, especially if it is in a place unaffected by hard frosts. However, harsh winds will

flowers attract bees but can snap the fragile stems, so be sure that the plant is staked and tied when necessary.

cause the leaves to blacken. It is common to see small standard bay trees outside restaurants in tubs or large pots, and they can be grown on a balcony. They need to be well watered and periodically dressed with manure or bone meal.

Bay leaves can be easily dried, or can be used straight from the tree, and as it is an evergreen there is little excuse not to use bay leaves all winter. Dried powdered bay leaves can be bought, but judge your quantities carefully if you use bay in this form as it's easy to use too much, which can result in a sour flavour.

5. Bergamot

Nearly all the herbs which have come to be used in English cooking since 1945 have had Mediterranean origins, so it is a surprise to discover that bergamot is associated with America, and as its leaves were grown to make infusions on the shores of Lake Oswego the plant is often known in the States as Oswego tea. It can grow to 1.2 m (4 ft), although 1 m (3 ft 3 in) is more usual, and it is happiest in deep shade and rich soil. Its small, bright red

It is best grown under a tree, for it beds down in winter under a blanket of leaves—peat can be used as a substitute if you have shade from another source. Allow the stems to grow brown and then cut the plant down to ground level in the autumn. Not only the leaves can be eaten but also the flowers, and many cooks sprinkle the bergamot blossom on salads, where it looks exotic and unusual. Bergamot leaves and blossom can also be dried and placed with ordinary tea in a canister to add a pungent, slightly antiseptic flavour. The sweet-smelling flowers and leaves are also used in pot pourris.

6. Borage

This is the great uplifter—from the Ancient Greeks to the Elizabethans it was used as a herb which raised spirits and created a sense of euphoria, but as we are now used to more potent pep pills, borage would probably seem a rather tame comforter today. However, it is still used in summer

digestion—indeed, some sufferers from indigestion like it in sandwiches rather than cucumber. A humble, low-growing herb, burnet has little or no smell and could easily be overlooked in a herb garden. Don't be tempted to grow it on for the sake of its flowers unless you want the seeds—the flowers are equally dull, and the herb loses some of its vigour and flavour after they have opened.

Burnet is very adaptable. It grows wild in many parts of England and can be placed in any type of soil.

drinks; a sprig of borage and a slice of cucumber are traditional not only in alcoholic drinks but also in lemonade and ginger ale.

Borage is an annual, but its seeds germinate easily and quickly and can be kept from one year to the next. Lucky gardeners may even find that their plants are self-seeding. The flowers, like those of bergamot, are edible and can be used in salads or crystallised; they are a romantic blue and can be very decorative. Tea infusions can be made from the leaves, which are also used to accompany salads. Borage leaves can be rather spiky until they have been washed, so take this precaution before using them. Some strawberry growers plant borage with their fruit—one plant seems to encourage the other.

7. Burnet

A friendly herb which grows best if several plants are placed together, burnet should only be used raw in salads. It is sometimes known as the cucumber herb for it tastes very like cucumber and can be an aid to

8. Chervil

If herbs are new to you chervil will become, with tarragon, your most amazing discovery. A tiny annual with no smell, it looks fragile and rather dull, but it has become one of the greatest assets in French cooking and you will need to grow a great deal of it, for it has its own soup which is one of the best flavours imaginable. However, it is a devil to grow outdoors for it likes semi-shade in summer and full sun in winter, and as it is best to plant a crop in late summer for early spring eating, you will see why your shade tree must be

deciduous—so that the sun can reach the chervil after the leaves have fallen.

Owing to its delicacy, chervil can be grown in pots and in a cool greenhouse or even on a window ledge, where you can give it the right amounts of light and shade. It is delicate to pluck too, as the roots are easily disturbed, so it should always be cut with scissors.

Grow some chervil plants for seed; it has a short life so keep sowing during the warm months to ensure a continuous supply. And sow as soon as you have the seed—like angelica, outdated chervil seed will not germinate. Once the plants are established cut them back when they begin to look leggy, to encourage a spriggy strong growth.

Chervil is often used as a more delicate substitute for parsley, but it is far superior as a garnish in salads, and with other herbs it can be used in omelettes or the classic Béarnaise sauce. It cannot be boiled, though, and should only be cooked very lightly—little more than heated through—to give the very best flavouring.

9. Chives

This well-known herb, a member of the onion family, has long bright green hollow stems flavoured with the most enchanting and restrained onion flavour. Chives are ideal for garnishes (unlike parsley, I can recommend this as their main use) and are also excellent snipped into salads or omelettes. Most slimmers know them as a dip with cottage cheese, which needs something to relieve the tedium.

Chives have very pretty flowers, but they do tend to dissipate the strength of the plant, so unless you grow some plants for decoration alone, it is wiser to keep your plants cut back. With care, they will spread, and as they are a vivid fresh green they can provide an agreeable swatch of emerald in the garden. Indeed, one famous French kitchen garden has a lawn of chives —which, of course, can only be clipped, not mown!

There is no reason why chives should not be grown from seed, but it is more satisfactory to grow from a root, and the clumps will divide very well after the first year's growth. Divide in the autumn and add plenty of manure to the soil; old coffee grounds are supposed to encourage chives too. It is almost imperative to divide the plants, as chives have an unhappy habit of dying for no apparent reason. As with all herbs, it is a good idea to keep a few understudy plants in the wings to replace the main clump if it fails. Chives must be cut regularly to promote growth, so ask a neighbour to help herself to this and other herbs while you are away on holiday—it's a kindness not only to your neighbour but also to your herb patch.

You may feel that there is no real necessity for a herb which is used mainly in garnishes or with cream cheese or omelettes, but the bounty of chives is widespread. It is available as early in the year as May, when its light, fresh flavour is very welcome. It can be grown in a pot, and is a pleasant and unusual addition to

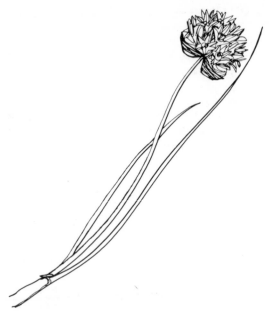

lightly braised in oil, water and lemon juice and put through a blender, and puréed comfrey leaves can also be added to tomato or carrot juice, as suggested in the excellent *Book of Herbs*.* As comfrey is extremely good for forming children's teeth, this might be a very good way to enable the family to benefit from it. Amazingly, comfrey will heal you on the inside or the outside, for the best natural cure for sprains, cuts or any lesions is a mixture of mashed leaves, either applied to the skin or swallowed!

The properties of comfrey don't stop there. If you want to use the roots they have the same cure-all properties as the leaves but in more intense quantities. Finally, and this may have most attraction for you, the plant is so bursting with goodness that it makes incredibly good compost, and is indeed grown agriculturally for this quality, so pick off any decaying comfrey leaves and dig them well into the rest of the herb garden and you will be providing the soil with nitrogen and calcium.

vinaigrette dressings, especially those used for cold meat, potato salads and hard-boiled eggs. Chives cannot be dried, but they can be frozen in plastic packets.

10. Comfrey

There is understandable nervousness about comfrey because the more extreme advocates of health cures do 'go on' about it. In fact they are absolutely right to be so enthusiastic, because comfrey is a great tissue healer and is also known as 'knit-bone' and 'boneset'. Not only those who believe in nature cures use it for treatment in T.B., ulcers and burns. Its product—allantoin—is used for cell replacement, and comfrey used in tisanes or as part of medicine goes into the blood to provide calcium and Vitamin B12.

In spite of these amazing properties, it is difficult to know how to use comfrey when you have it in the garden, as the leaves are quite coarse when raw. If you have enough plants, the big leaves can be added to spinach and cooked into a purée. Or try cooking them in batter. They can be

The Book of Herbs by Dorothy Hall (Pan).

And of course the roots do the same service, so that as the plant spreads underground, delving very deeply, and a good deal lower than the rest of your herbs, the decaying older roots will send up a continual supply of goodness to the plants above. Comfrey is perennial.

11. Dill

Unfortunately dill is an annual, but in a sheltered position it may seed itself. It is the most popular herb in Scandinavia, where it is used in fish and potato cookery. Like many herbs it has a twofold use; its leaves have a light aniseed flavour, and the seeds are stronger and more similar to caraway. It does not dry happily, but it can be frozen quite easily in plastic packets or in ice cubes. Lovers of pickled cucumbers and gherkins will recognise dill as the main flavouring, and in Eastern Europe and Russia it is used in sour-cream dishes and sauces. It can also be used as an accompaniment to new potatoes, and dill vinegar can be made simply by placing a spray of dill in a bottle of vinegar. If you think of dill as a natural accompaniment to sour dishes you will have a good idea of its properties.

If you grow both dill and fennel, label them and leave a gap between them for one plant can be mistaken for another. In fact dill is a more refined shape, but both have feathery leaves and wide-seeded heads like miniature cow parsley. Dill is fairly hardy but cannot withstand cold winds.

12. Fennel

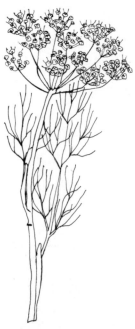

A double-acting herb, fennel can be grown as a vegetable as well as a flavouring. Florence fennel is cultivated for its root, a strong aniseed-tasting growth like bulbous celery, which can be grated or thinly sliced in a salad or else steamed and eaten with cheese sauce as a vegetable in winter. However, in the limited area of a herb garden you will wish to grow sweet fennel for its leaves and seeds. These look very

This fennel plant has been pruned to an ornamental shape. Its flower heads will provide seeds for use in herb bread; the thin fragrant leaves are strewn on fish, and when the flower dies back the twiggy old stems make an excellent fire on which to grill fish

like dill, but the plant is rather more vigorous and a little taller.

Fennel leaves are used with all oily fish; in Italy the dried twiggy hollow stems are also burnt under bass or tuna so that the fish is impregnated with the fennel flavour. When the flowers are dead the dried seeds can be used; sprinkle them on bread or into rolls.

Traditionally fennel seeds abated hunger, and could still be chewed before meals if you wished to slim! Infusions of fennel leaves were restoratives for eye diseases and failing sight.

Florence fennel, the bulbous-rooted vegetable, is an annual, but sweet fennel, grown for its leaves and seeds, is a perennial.

13. Geranium

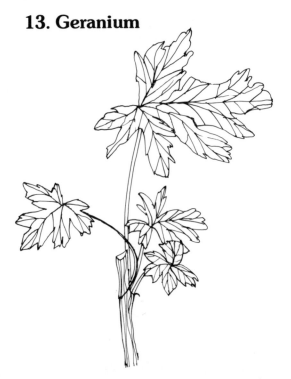

It may seem surprising to suggest a popular flower as a herb, but like roses, violets, nasturtiums and japonica, geraniums have a place in the kitchen as well as the flower border. They should not be left out all winter, but can be taken out of the garden and either put in a pot to spend a retired winter indoors, or dried and allowed to remain in a dark, cool but frost-free store until the spring, when leaves will begin to shoot again.

Scented-leaved geraniums have insignificant flowers, either white or pale lilac, but they are grown for their leaves which are graceful, plentiful and very sweetly scented, especially if you rub them between your fingers. The scents vary greatly, and each adds a certain flavour of its smell to dishes to which it is added. For instance, lemon geranium may be used in lemon snow or lemon custards, and rose geranium in cakes where rosewater would be used; peppermint dishes can be made from the beautiful 'tomentosum', which has soft velvety leaves smelling and tasting of peppermint. There is also an apple geranium and the common 'quercifolium', or oak-leaved, geranium, which can flavour stews and casseroles. Geranium ice cream is yet another treat. Cuttings can be taken from geraniums very easily, so they can be used as unusual presents, and the dried leaves are splendid additions to pot pourri. Finally, as the oily smells alienate slugs they are excellent edging plants, and may stop pests reaching your other herbs.

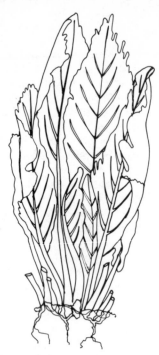

there is hardly any need to worry about propagation!

Dry the roots in a cool oven. If you use gas and have a perpetual pilot light the heat should be enough, but do not allow them to become too dry—they should only be brittle enough to grate. If you wish to keep the root flexible, store it in white wine vinegar. Horseradish is not only delightful with beef; one of the best sauces for baked trout is made of grated horseradish, walnuts and sour cream.

15. Hyssop

14. Horseradish

It's ironic that those of us who have established horseradish plants spend all our time trying to eradicate them, while those who have none are prepared to pay extravagant prices for the shredded fresh roots. Once you have planted this gregarious root it will take over the garden unless you are strict about digging up roots which stray beyond the boundaries you have decided for it. It looks very like dock leaves when young, and can easily be discarded as a weed. If your garden is large enough, plant horseradish and comfrey a little apart from the main herb garden, so that they can multiply without taking over the soil, unless you want to keep comfrey as a soil enricher.

Horseradish has a unique flavour, immediately hot in the mouth but then cooling, and in Britain it is best known as an accompaniment to roast beef. The root can go well down into the ground searching for rich soil; when you dig up your first plant, retain the main tap root and replant the small side roots to form strong parent plants the next year. However,

Another herb for nostalgia, for we rarely use hyssop today. It is a perennial which is very quickly grown from seed, and then can be divided. Its main function in a herb garden today is as an attraction for bees and butterflies, so keep it in the sunlight and in a part of the border where less conspicuous flowers can benefit from its visitors. It is not used much in British cooking. Hyssop can be used externally and internally as a medicine, for it relieves catarrh when made into a tisane, and if it is heated in a sachet and applied to the skin it can heal a black eye.

16. Juniper

Juniper provides height (1.2–1.5 m—4–5 ft) for the herb garden, a certain amount of shade for low-lying plants and a berry for casseroles and game dishes. You will need patience, for the berries take three years to ripen and can only be used when they are purple-black; however, as with figs, new berries form each year so that there will be a succession of fruit after the first crop.

Juniper will grow in almost any conditions, its natural habitat being rocky hillsides, but sun is needed to ripen the berries. A horizontal juniper can be used to screen parts of the garden, especially septic-tank covers, rubbish or manure heaps, but this is not the berry-producing bush, which is called *juniperus communis*.

The tree or bush makes a pretty and distinctive background in a border as it is evergreen, and looks particularly handsome behind silvery plants. As only female bushes are fruit-bearing you may have some disappointment in growing juniper, but if you have an opportunity to buy an established bush you can ascertain if it has berries or not.

Northern climates result in a less flavoured berry and if you follow Mediterranean receipes you may need more home-grown berries than the amount specified. Oil of juniper is a base for gin, and it is this pine flavour which adds so much to game, ham and beef dishes. Crush the berry before adding it.

17. Lavender

This is one of the most notable plants in a herb garden, but its kitchen qualities are negligible.

Lavender oil is an antiseptic and an insect deterrent, so it can be most useful in warm climates. The flower is supreme in pot pourri and lavender sachets for scenting linen cupboards, so perhaps we can hardly expect much more of it, but do remember it when drying underwear, and spread your washing over the tops of the bushes on a sunny day.

18. Lovage

This is another herb which will be a continual and unexpected pleasure. It is grown too rarely, and you will probably have to buy a plant from a specialist grower. It will look dwarfish to begin with, but given rich earth and light lovage may be one of the tallest plants in the herb garden, so leave it plenty of room.

When added to stews or other cooked dishes lovage has a strong yeasty flavour, but it is best in a salad where its celery-like taste, when raw, is refreshing and unusual. It has, almost more than any herb, the quality of tasting fresh and of the country, and visitors will love it. Use it

liberally once you are accustomed to it, for lovage also has strong deodorant qualities!

If you have to grow it from seed you will find that it takes a long time to germinate; as with parsley, it is easy to give up, and throw out the compost in despair! But persevere with seeds if you cannot find plants. Well-manured soil will help this herb immensely; it grows deeply but slowly so it will benefit from compost dug into the earth before planting.

19. Marjoram

This is a confusing herb. There are several branches of the family and each varies a little and has a different name: there are sweet and pot marjoram, and the continental oregano—take your pick.

You will discover that oregano, which is a wild marjoram, has a coarser and stronger flavour suitable for Italian cooking. The British-based marjorams are sweeter and fainter.

Sweet marjoram has a better flavour but is an annual, which will suffer from the

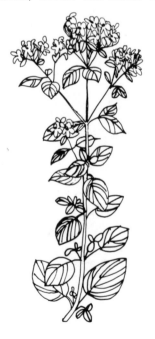

One of the most useful herbs, lovage makes a good soup and can be eaten raw on salads. A small plant may grow to fill a large space in the herb garden

first frost; pot marjoram will survive the cold weather and may last for many years, and may be propagated most successfully by division. It has a more acrid flavour which can hold its own with flavours such as onion and garlic, and is therefore commonly used in stuffings or casseroles. Sometimes the plant is known as knotted marjoram owing to the tight furled buds, which should be removed as flowering detracts from the flavour of the leaves, though of course the plant can be encouraged to flower for seed.

Like basil, which it resembles, marjoram is very good for tomato dishes, and for meat recipes. To really get the best out of the herb, fold it into scones or dumplings to simmer in the top of a stew where it will impart its oily pungent flavour to both the dough and the meat. Clippings of the leaves can be added to bread and scones, and you may like to experiment by using it instead of thyme in stuffing. The distinctive flavour encountered in Italian home cooking is often owed to oregano, but cultivated marjoram can be an effective substitute if it is used more plentifully. Marjoram can also be added to pot pourri.

20. Mint

Pernicious and insidious mint—it is perhaps the most commonly used herb in British cooking, yet few gardeners have a kind word to say about the plant. Once let it get established in a flowerbed and it will take over the garden—an attractive tyrant, it is true, for it has pale mauve flowers and a delicious scent, but a tyrant nonetheless, for its roots will creep along underground and attempt to throttle every other plant nearby. What is the answer? Plant it in a pot sunk into the herb patch and you can control its voracity. Some lovers of mint go further and plant their favourite mints in an old tin bath with holes punched in the bottom. Don't be afraid that this will look ugly—in any herb garden it will be

masked in one season, and if the mint crawls over the side it will soon look like a leafy boulder. Mint does need a moist position, and if you have a stream or pool in the garden it can look very graceful growing by the edge. It also needs sunlight to bring out the flavour, so do not attempt to grow mint in a woodland setting.

There are three types of mint which are usually grown: garden mint (a round-leafed variety), apple mint, which has a faint fruity flavour, and Eau de Cologne mint, which is harder to come by but has an added attraction in that it scents the kitchen when cooked with any vegetable. Other possible varieties are spearmint, the smallest and most compact of the mints, which can be grown in a flower-pot indoors; Bowles mint; and peppermint. The last two are taller than spearmint but have more flavour. If space is limited, choose a variety other than common mint for the garden. Apple mint is perhaps the most useful, and also the easiest to buy. Mint cannot easily be grown from seed, but most gardeners will be glad to reduce their plots by giving you a root or a cutting.

TYPE OF OIL	SUGGESTED USE	DOUCHE/SITZBATH	BATH OIL	VAPORIZATION	PERFUMES	INHALATION	COMPRESS	MASSAGE OILS	SUITABLE FOR
BASIL	MEDICINAL		B			I	C		TENSION, NERVES, FAINTING, MIGRAINE (LIGHT COMPRESS ON THE TEMPLES)
	MOOD CHANGE		B	V		I			DEPRESSION, MENTAL FATIGUE, POOR MEMORY
BERGAMOT •	MEDICINAL	D/S	B						HALITOSIS, CYSTITIS, COLD SORES, BODY ODOURS.
	MOOD CHANGE		B	V					DEPRESSION, TENSION
	BEAUTY CARE							M	ACNE, SKIN OIL FOR NIGHT USE ONLY
CEDARWOOD	MEDICINAL		B			I			CATARRH, BREATHING CONGESTION
	MOOD CHANGE		B	V					TENSION
	BEAUTY CARE							M	ACNE, OILY SKIN
CLARY SAGE •	MEDICINAL		B	V			C	M	PERIOD PAINS, INSOMNIA, BODY ODOUR
	MOOD CHANGE		B	V	P			M	DEPRESSION, ALSO AN APHRODISIAC
	BEAUTY CARE							M	ALL SKIN TYPES, ESPECIALLY OVER-HYDRATED SKIN, CELLULITIS
CYPRESS •	MEDICINAL	D/S	B			I			COUGHS, PILES, BODY ODOUR, VARICOSE VEINS
	MOOD CHANGE		B	V					RELAXATION (SOOTHING, REFRESHING)
	BEAUTY CARE							M	OILY SKIN
EUCALYPTUS •	MEDICINAL			V		I	C	M	CATARRH, NASAL CONGESTION, COLD SORES, DIARRHOEA, ACHES AND PAINS
FRANKINCENSE •	MEDICINAL		B	V		I		M	CATARRH, RHEUMATIC PAINS
	MOOD CHANGE		B	V					MEDITATION, RELAXATION (SOOTHING, WARMING)
	BEAUTY CARE						C	M	REJUVENATION OF MATURE SKIN
GERANIUM •	MEDICINAL		B	V					TENSION, NERVES, WOUNDS & CUTS (APPLY DIRECT TO PART AFFECTED)
	MOOD CHANGE		B	V					BALANCING EMOTIONS (DEPRESSION/OVER STIMULATION)
	BEAUTY CARE							M	DRY SKIN, COMBINATION SKIN
JUNIPER •	MEDICINAL	D/S	B	V				M	OBESITY, FLUID RETENTION, POOR CIRCULATION, CYSTITIS
	MOOD CHANGE		B	V					HYPERTENSION
	BEAUTY CARE							M	ACNE, OILY SKIN
LAVENDER •	MEDICINAL	D/S	B	V			C	M	HEADACHE, INSOMNIA, BURNS, WOMEN'S PROBLEMS, REDUCING SCAR TISSUE
	MOOD CHANGE		B	V	P			M	ANXIETY, EXHAUSTION, HYPERTENSION
	BEAUTY CARE						C	M	REJUVENATION OF MATURE SKIN, OILY SKIN
LEMON •	MEDICINAL		B	V			C		INDIGESTION, HEADACHE, CHILBLAINS
	MOOD CHANGE		B	V					REFRESHING (GENTLY UPLIFTING)
	BEAUTY CARE							M	ACNE, OILY SKIN
LEMONGRASS •	MEDICINAL		B	V					INDIGESTION, NERVOUS TENSION, STRESS DISORDERS
	MOOD CHANGE		B	V				M	BALANCING EMOTIONS (DEPRESSION/HYPERTENSION)
	BEAUTY CARE							M	OILY SKIN
MARJORAM	MEDICINAL		B	V			C		INSOMNIA, MIGRAINE, BRUISES, CRAMP, RHEUMATIC PAINS
	MOOD CHANGE		B	V					ANXIETY, SEDATIVE
ORANGE •	MEDICINAL		B	V					INSOMNIA
	MOOD CHANGE		B	V					TIREDNESS, MENTAL FATIGUE
	BEAUTY CARE							M	OILY SKIN
PATCHOULI •	MEDICINAL		B					M	SCAR TISSUE, NERVOUS TENSION
	MOOD CHANGE		B	V	P			M	DEPRESSION, ANXIETY, ALSO AN APHRODISIAC
	BEAUTY CARE							M	MATURE OR DRY SKIN
PEPPERMINT	MEDICINAL		B			I	C		INDIGESTION, TRAVEL SICKNESS, NAUSEA, MIGRAINE
	MOOD CHANGE			V					OVER-STIMULATION
ROSEMARY •	MEDICINAL		B	V			C		FATIGUE, ARTHRITIS, CIRCULATORY PROBLEMS, 'HANGOVERS'
	MOOD CHANGE		B	V		I			APATHY, RESTORING NERVOUS BALANCE, TIREDNESS
	BEAUTY CARE		B						FACIAL WASH, CLEANSING HAIR RINSE (DILUTED IN WATER)
ROSEWOOD •	MEDICINAL		B	V					INSOMNIA
	MOOD CHANGE		B	V		I			ANXIETY
	BEAUTY CARE							M	DRY SKIN, HAIR RINSE FOR DRY HAIR (DILUTED IN WATER)
SANDALWOOD •	MEDICINAL		B				C	M	SORE THROAT
	MOOD CHANGE		B	V	P				MEDITATION, RELAXATION (CALMING)
	BEAUTY CARE							M	ACNE, DRY SKIN
TEA TREE •	MEDICINAL	D/S	B				C		CUTS, COLD SORES, SORE THROATS (GARGLE), THRUSH, MOUTH ULCERS
	BEAUTY CARE							M	ACNE (USE NEAT ON BOILS AND SPOTS)
YLANG-YLANG •	MEDICINAL		B	V				M	NERVOUS TENSION
	MOOD CHANGE		B	V	P				ANXIETY, DEPRESSION, ALSO AN APHRODISIAC
	BEAUTY CARE							M	OILY SKIN, DRY SKIN, COMBINATION SKIN

essential oils are ideal air fresheners

Thes

Apple mint—this prolific plant is very useful if it is kept within bounds! The flavour is more delicate than that of common mint

It is amazing how many more uses there are for mint than as a flavouring for peas and new potatoes, or mint sauce and mint jelly with lamb, delicious though these are. The secret of mint is that it can be used with sweet and savoury dishes. Also mints are good additions to summer drinks, and iced tea absolutely demands a handful of crushed mint leaves to go with each jug. Both the smell and the taste of mint are so redolent of hot summer days that it isn't surprising to find mint as a staple ingredient in many Near Eastern dishes, and in chilled soups. Consider, too, mint leaves on salads, with fruit salads and strawberries, in sandwiches, and embedded in lime or lemon jelly.

Mint makes a sweet-smelling and attractive decoration too; a large bowl will fill a drawing-room with intense perfume, and as the stems are stiff but the leaves lax it is easy to arrange. Mint dries well but becomes extremely strong in flavour, so take care to use smaller quantities than those suggested in recipes incorporating fresh sprigs. Dried mint leaves are an invaluable addition to pot pourri, and make delicious tisanes or herb teas.

21. Parsley

This is one of the herbs which is so popular that it is available in many greengrocers' shops, and it has become almost obligatory on boiled potatoes in many restaurants where other herbs are inadmissible. Robert Landry, a French cookery writer, is scathing: 'It lends itself to the worst hustling of pseudo-gastronomic restaurants and permits housewives to imagine that they really know aromatic botany.' This is unkind, for parsley is a necessity in *bouquet garni*, where the stalks add as much flavour as the leaves.

Parsley comes in various forms, and if you have a vegetable garden you can become much more expansive with this herb,

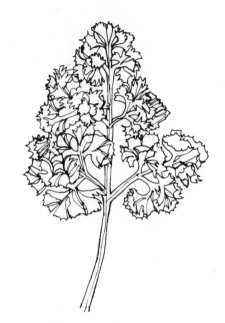

growing it as a border to rows of vegetables or even planting a row of Hamburg parsley, which is too little known in Britain, although it was a common vegetable before the Industrial Revolution.

The most common parsley in this country is curly-leaved, which looks more decorative than the plain-leaved varieties found on the Continent. Though it is the standby of every cook who wishes her vegetables or grilled meat to look more appetising, it should not be confined to the role of garnish, where it is often pushed to the side of the plate and discarded. Parsley is full of Vitamin C, and can be eaten in a variety of guises. When chopped finely with shallots it forms persillade, which should be added to dishes at the last minute so that its flavour stays sharp and fresh. It can be made into parsley butter or fried, forming an unusual accompaniment to fish dishes.

Hamburg parsley is one of those useful herbs which are edible in every part, having a long tapering root like common parsley but with a spicier flavour, nearer to celeriac. It is excellent as the base of a casserole or braising dish, imparting a more unusual flavour than the commonly used turnip or carrot. It can also be braised in butter and stock and served as a vegetable, or added as a purée to soup. In fact, use Hamburg parsley roots as if they were parsnips. The leaves are not used so often, but I prefer their slightly iodine-tasting flavour to ordinary parsley, and they can be sprinkled whole, in small amounts, into salads.

There are gadgets on the market which will chop parsley or mint, but not only do they squeeze the juice out, they are the devil to clean. An experienced cook often prefers to chop parsley on a board with a sharp straight-bladed French kitchen knife, or in a wooden bowl with a curved knife (an *hachinette*).

Parsley is a biennial, so you will need to plant two patches in the garden, to ensure that some is available every year. Once it is established, parsley will flourish, especially if it is in slight shade and with deep well-manured soil, but it seems to take an age to germinate and I have known many gardeners start parsley off in a seedbox, despair at the lack of results and throw the whole lot out! Germination can be speeded up if you keep the seeds in your freezer for a few weeks before sowing them.

Parsley does not mind the confinement of windowsill culture, and this is a good way of keeping it going through the winter; alternatively, sow a patch outside in early autumn.

Don't dismiss parsley; its medicinal virtues alone (traditionally it relieves rheumatism) should make it a basic herb in any kitchen—but do remove it from the restriction of a garnish!

22. Pennyroyal

This is a mint which is not especially recommended for use in the kitchen, for its flavour is usually too emphatic to be used as a mint substitute. However, it does thwart insects, especially ants, and a fringe

of pennyroyal round your herb garden will help to free the plot from pests.

Owing to this deterrent value it is often a good idea to scatter a few leaves of pennyroyal in a dog's blankets or basket, to ward off fleas; a judicious application of crushed leaves can even be used instead of flea powder, rubbed it into the animal's coat if the skin is healthy.

Pennyroyal flourishes in the most stony soil, so it can be planted in crazy paving, again eliminating ants, and as it seems to send out some leaves in winter, it can be used very sparingly to flavour potatoes or peas—but be very mean with pennyroyal, it can be too pungent. Like mints in general it prefers damp ground, but this is not vital for its survival.

23. Rosemary

Rosemary is another herb against which you may be biased because it is often over-used. Some cooks saturate their lamb dishes with this spiky, oily herb, which can permeate the meat and destroy its flavour. Rosemary, like sage and thyme, should be

used to underline the fresh pure taste of food, not to overwhelm it with its own unique aroma.

So always use rosemary with a hesitant touch, and try to find sprigs which are sappy and won't come to pieces in the food but which can be removed whole before the dish reaches the table. Remember that some people do not like the camphorous pine flavour at all, so do not add rosemary to meals destined for guests until you are sure it will be appreciated.

However, rosemary is an essential herb for cooks, not only to flavour lamb but also to go with other meats, including pork, and vegetables. It can be used in winter as a substitute for thyme, because it is evergreen. This also means that there is little necessity to use powdered or dried forms of the herb. In any case, powdered rosemary is almost too strong, and easy to use to excess, and dried rosemary can be a prickly subject, for the needles will spike the meat so successfully that your guests will be picking them out of their teeth for hours after the meal.

Rosemary has other uses apart from cookery. It is an attractive bushy plant which can be cut for decoration, and also has a great reputation as a beauty aid. Rosemary infusions can be used as a hairwash, and it is often used to scent shampoos and soaps. A little concentrated oil of rosemary rubbed into the scalp leaves the hair shining and silky, though very often commercially prepared rosemary shampoos seem to have a drying effect.

Although it can make a pretty hedge or border edging, rosemary does not always grow well in Britain. Like many plants which flourish in the Mediterranean, it loses some of its aroma and strength in a colder climate, and an attempt to grow it in northern England could well end in disappointment. It is very prone to damage from high winds and frosts, but if you have a sunny, stony, sheltered situation, though they are often hard to find in this country, that is where to plant your rosemary bush. If it does settle it can grow for over twenty years, and might reach the 2 m (6 ft 6 in) often seen in Corsican and Italian bushes.

Rosemary needs little pruning, unless it starts to look unattractively leggy; often, continual plucking for the kitchen will keep a bush in trim. Rosemary is a good basic shrub for the general garden. It is most valuable for its foliage, which forms a year-round deep blue-green background for smaller light, feathery plants, and it also bears pretty lilac flowers in late June and early July.

24. Sage

Pungent, even acrid, sage is not always popular with experienced cooks, and indeed its flavour can be very strong and overpowering if it is used unwisely. Its very strength sets it apart from other herbs with their delicate, flowery tastes. You will either love it or hate it; if the former, you may find that some of the other herbs mentioned here are too weak for your palate.

Perhaps because of the great popularity

bush fails it is worth trying again with a different variety. It should be propagated by cuttings, which take easily.

Although dried and powdered sage is common, it is not a herb which can be dried very successfully as it loses some flavour, so if you have a healthy bush try to use fresh leaves as often as possible. The young sprigs, which have tender stems, can be cooked with peas and beans for an unusual flavour, and try the tender topbuds on green salad. Rub tiny specks of sage leaves into cream cheese or add a spoonful of chopped leaves to the sauce for a Welsh rarebit and you will be pleased to find a whole new repertoire for this mis-used and argumentative herb.

25. Savory

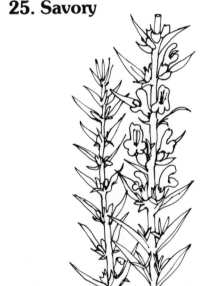

of sage and onion stuffing, sage has remained generally popular in British cooking when other, more useful herbs have lost countenance. It is a favourite flavouring for sausages and pork products generally, though on the Continent it succeeds best in Italian veal dishes, where it is combined simply with the veal and white wine. Indeed, sage rarely appears with other herbs because it does not accord happily with any other flavour.

Sage is very decorative in the garden, where the tapering, velvety, soft grey-green leaves make a handsome backcloth for shorter herbs. The purple flowers, larger and more decorative than most herb blossoms, often make the biggest splash of colour in a herb border. Sage bushes, which can become large and woody, like a well-drained position and plenty of sun. Even if you cannot supply these, make sure sage is not in a damp place, for many bushes die from overwatering or wet roots. Although most nurserymen do not realise it, there are various different types of sage, including narrow-leaved, broad-leaved and purely decorative varieties. If your sage

There are two main savories, the winter and summer varieties. Summer savory has a better flavour but is an annual, and many gardeners prefer to plant winter savory, which is a perennial and shrubby, with stronger growth. The flavour is rather like thyme, and it can be substituted for it, which is useful in winter when evergreen savory comes into its own in the kitchen. In France savory is the usual accompaniment to broad beans and in Germany it flavours trout, and it is also used on the Continent in sausages. A more recent use is as an addition to *sautéed* courgettes.

Fortunately, savory is not over-fussy about its habitat although it prefers a sunny position. Given a good place in the herb garden you might find that summer savory is self-seeding.

26. Sorrel

This is a vegetable rather than a herb and could be grown in rows very successfully, but unless you are an addict of sorrel soup you might find that one or two tall, healthy plants will supply a family with enough to flavour sauces for fish, veal or eggs.

Although it is officially a 'sour dock', don't think that you can collect wild sorrel and achieve the same results as by using French sorrel, planted from a cultivated root or sown from seed. The larger variety, also called Herb Patience, can grow to prodigious heights for a herb, and should

be planted at the back of the garden, but the more common French sorrel is smaller, reaching 0.75–1 m (2 ft 6 in–3 ft 3 in).

Cook it in an enamel pan—never in iron, which combines with the sorrel to form a black metallic vegetable—and for similar reasons cut it with a stainless-steel bladed knife. There is so much oxalic acid in sorrel that it can be harmful, but taken in small doses sorrel is a first-rate provider of Vitamin C.

The most customary use of sorrel is as a flavouring for sauce to go with white fish, or as a vegetable *purée* with fish. Its bitter flavour is a delight to the gourmet. It looks like spinach and should be cooked in the same way, lightly, and in the water which is left on the leaves after washing. Many cooks add a little sorrel to spinach, in order to give the other vegetable a more exotic flavour.

27. Sweet Cicely

This herb would not have had a prominent place in any herbal until recent years, for it

Not to be taken by those with kidney disorders, sorrel can become a valuable 'fillip' in a green sauce for fish, or as a sour addition to spinach. It makes an excellent soup

is a sugar provider, and as such had very little culinary interest. However, there has been such propaganda concerning the harm done by white sugar, and also we are so figure-conscious nowadays, that Sweet Cicely is suddenly promoted from being an old-fashioned plant grown for sentimental reasons, into being a provider of sweetness for fruit dishes. It's a perennial, smelling and tasting rather like aniseed, and in the past the root was also eaten, cooked like celeriac and then grated, with a salad dressing.

The use of Sweet Cicely will not eliminate the need for sugar, but the amount of sugar can be halved when stewing sour fruit. Diabetics have known its properties for many years and it will be interesting to see if Sweet Cicely comes back into favour with the rest of us. The leaves can also be sprinkled over salad, or added to summer drinks.

Apart from all this attraction as a herb, Sweet Cicely is a pretty plant which could be put in a herbaceous border, and it has a long period of use, for the leaves appear early and can remain until late November or even, in a mild area, early December.

28. Tarragon

There are certain herbs which give one such delight in discovery that they become favourites in the herb garden, and tarragon is one of these; indeed, some cooks say that if only one herb were available it should be tarragon. It has fewer uses than thyme or parsley, but its unique flavour is so enchanting that few of us who love tarragon could be without it. Unfortunately it is expensive and does not grow happily from seed, so it has to be bought from a specialist grower. Try to buy French tarragon. The more common Russian variety is less well flavoured, but it will certainly do if the French sort is unobtainable—even the great restaurants of Paris often have to resort to the imported variety. Country

cooks are usually more fortunate in obtaining true French *estragon*.

It is part of the family of artemisia, which are staple herbs in the garden, for although they are not mentioned in this list, both southernwood and wormwood are excellent also-rans for the border, with a delicious and unique fragrance; however, these cousins of tarragon have little culinary value unless you wish to make absinthe, and so they are not included here.

French cooking, both *haute cuisine* and regional, relies enormously on this herb. It appears in sauces, egg and fish dishes, and soups; it is the basis for sauce Béarnaise, the most commonly used herb with roast chicken, and if a sprig is added to wine vinegar, after two or three months the aromatic vinegar can be used in salad dressings. However, use tarragon sparingly until you are accustomed to it, for its unusual flavour, both bitter and sweet, can

leave an aftertaste of which many people are wary.

Once you have become accustomed to it you will find that tarragon is the most enchanting herb in the garden; but be careful in growing it. It does not grow easily from seed and it costs a lot, so buy a bushy plant if you can, and take rootlet cuttings as soon as possible so that you have substitute plants—you can always give them away if necessary. Shelter the parent plant, for frost, cold winds and damp soil are all anathema to tarragon. I have always kept it in pots even when the plant is quite large, and either brought them in for winter, or else put them on a bench or raised bricks in a warm corner near a wall which will reflect what sunshine is available.

29. Thyme

Thyme is such a well-known and easily activated herb that some enthusiasts put it into every dish. In reaction to this over-use, more serious cooks often go too far in the other direction, and neglect it. But did you know that thyme is also a very powerful antiseptic and is used in medicines? In a recent study of herbs and their curative values, it is said that no bacilli can withstand the action of thyme essence for more than thirty-five or forty minutes, and thymol is used as a base for cough medicines.

There are many types of thyme; common thyme or lemon thyme are the best for cooking. The latter is a shorter plant than the former, 150 mm (6 in) tall as opposed to 300 mm (12 in), and it has a more flowery flavour. Its leaves are pale gold and form a wide rosette shape; they can be chopped and sprinkled onto salads. In theory lemon thyme should do well in pots, but in fact it seems to lack the toughness of common thyme. Two other unusually flavoured varieties of thyme are caraway thyme, which comes from Sardinia and Corsica, and orange thyme.

Thyme has a pungent taste and smell, and should be used sparingly with other herbs. It does, however, combine with bay, parsley and rosemary, to make *bouquet garni*. It is much used in Mediterranean cooking, appearing in many meat dishes, and it can also be added profitably to chicken, fish, soups, stews and casseroles. Writers rhapsodise about the wild thyme of the Mediterranean hillsides, declaring it to be superior in flavour to that which is grown in the back garden. Personally I have found the wild thyme of Provence a little disappointing, although one of the best meals I have ever eaten in Southern France was lamb cutlets brought to the table on an iron tray on which thyme cuttings blazed below the meat.

Thyme is a delightful herb to grace any garden, supplying a variety of very pleasing fragrances as well as attractive foliage; two particularly decorative varieties are shepherd's thyme, which is grown mainly in cracks between paving-stones, and is like a small pincushion in shape, and silver thyme, which makes a valuable contribution to the colour variations of any flowerbed.

Once established, thyme grows happily and can keep going for years. Common garden or 'black' thyme benefits from cropping, though, as it can become rather leggy. It has pinky-cream flowers in June, but should be cut back for drying during May. Thyme keeps better than almost any other herb, drying very well and also freezing successfully. To dry, hang the twigs in a shady place for a week or so, and when it is dry, rub the leaves from the twigs and store them in airtight jars. However, any fresh thyme is better than the dried variety and you may find that your thyme plants produce a few leaves even in winter; if not, savory is a good substitute, so storing may be unnecessary.

Thyme can be used to flavour olive oil and vinegar, and as a constituent of herb cushions, pot pourri and thyme tea.

30. Verbena

Do not confuse verbena with vervain, another member of the same family which was used in the past in country medicines. Lemon verbena is a sweetly scented herb

and can be used almost everywhere that lemon fragrance and flavour are desired. However, it is not usually a culinary herb, but is grown for its place in pot pourris; indeed, its lemony tang can be rather off-putting in cooking as it may sometimes smell of sickly soap.

It is occasionally used, however, for flavouring custards and creams. Lemon verbena can take the place of the lemon grass flavour used in curries and in Indonesian cookery, and some cooks use a leaf of lemon verbena instead of lemon zest in *mousses* or *soufflés* when bottled lemon juice is used instead of fresh fruit. The French make a verbena tea which is supposedly soothing to frazzled nerves; however, as almost any herbal tisane would serve, it might be better to use a more common herb for a tisane and keep your lemon verbena for sweet puddings and fragrance.

Verbena will attract bees, and although it is a perennial plant it will suffer in frosts and would benefit if it were potted and brought indoors or into a cold greenhouse in the winter.

5 ～ Preserving Herbs

Probably every herb is better fresh than preserved, and if you have a successful herb garden you will always have some sprigs which can be used in winter or else a few plants which are being cared for indoors. Annuals, especially basil, present the greatest problem, but you will have read in the last chapter that even this can be fostered in the winter. However, it is just as well to have a reserve of dried or frozen herbs, which can be used if plants fail, or which can be given away to friends.

Dried herbs don't last for ever, and a fresh stock should be made each year. Drying concentrates the flavour of the herbs, so it is customary to use a third of the quantity required for fresh leaves. Because of this, make sure that you know if the recipe you are using stipulates fresh or dried herbs; most recipes suggest dried herbs as these are more commonly used. In changing from dried to fresh herbs you will probably have to experiment to suit your own taste.

Freezing

Most of your renewal of preserved herbs will take place in May, before the flowering season but after the fresh spring growth has been established. What you freeze depends on what you use most, but thyme, marjoram, tarragon and parsley are almost essential, and you can also freeze *bouquets garnis*. Make sure that all herbs are well

Put pinches of chopped parsley or mint in ice cube moulds, cover with water and freeze

insulated in the freezer, for they will smell more strongly than most frozen food and if any scent or flavour seeps out it can pervade the compartment. Apart from parsley, do not freeze herbs which you wish to use raw, only those to be used in cooking.

Parsley and mint should be chopped into small pieces and frozen in water in ice-cube trays. Afterwards, remove the cubes and store them in plastic bags; when you need them remove a cube at a time. The ice keeps the herb fresh and you will rarely need less than the amount of leaves you can pack into one cube. Parsley frozen in this way can be used raw, as a garnish; and it is a herb which is better frozen than dried. It can also be frozen whole, as with other herbs; unlike them, however, the stems, which are edible, can be included.

Freeze the herbs in jars, which should be absolutely airtight; tiny honey pots, used herb jars and small Marmite jars are the most useful sizes. Remove the leaves from the stems, pack the jars and use them to fill the side pockets of your freezing area when you are freezing larger packs of food. A small amount can be removed from the jars when it is needed.

Bouquets garnis freeze very successfully. These bunches of rosemary, thyme, bay leaf and parsley can be tied with nylon thread or sewing cotton and placed in a screwtop jar, quite a large one this time; store them in the door of the freezer once they have been frozen, if you have an upright model.

Bouquet garni

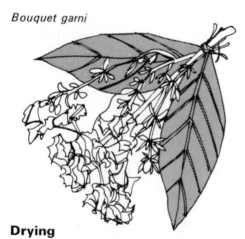

Drying

Pick the herbs on a warm day in May, in the morning before the sun is too strong. They can be dried out of doors in very hot weather, although this is a chancy business owing to bird droppings and cats. If you do wish to dry them this way, make a screen by stretching nylon net curtain over a frame. This can be an old box to which the net can be tacked, or—if you use a cardboard box—taped. Spread the herbs over the net, so that the air can circulate underneath them, and pray that it won't rain. Don't leave the herbs outside at night,

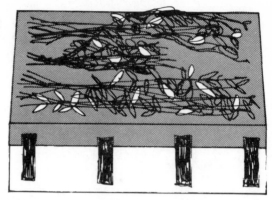

Spread herbs to dry in the open air on an old net curtain taped to the open side of a box

as they could be affected by dew.

It is more usual to dry herbs indoors. You need dry weather, to retain the rich oils which must be preserved in the herbs. They can be dried in bunches hanging in a draught, or else spread out on sheets of paper in a warm dry place. Before you make up the bunches, be sure that you can identify each herb as the leaves will shrivel and may be unrecognisable; reliance on smell and taste is usually not enough. It will take a week or so to dry the herbs, but inspect them daily as the drying period varies according to conditions. They will be ready when they have changed colour and are fairly dry but not too brittle.

Herbs can also be dried in an oven at low heat, spread on sheets of foil. This is an easy method but not very good for the herbs as the heat often extracts the oils.

When they are ready for picking, cover a table with white paper (lining paper for shelves will do, or newspaper, although the print can confuse the eye). Have ready as many airtight jars as you have types of herb and make sure each one is labelled before you begin. It is a good idea to add the date to each label. Darkened glass or earthenware containers will preserve the herbs for longer than clear glass ones, but even so they should not be used after two years. Now strip the leaves off the stalks— they will come away easily when dry.

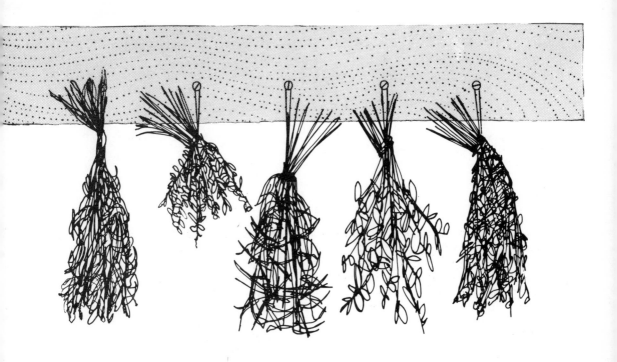

You may find that you often need special mixtures, for soup or fish or beef dishes for instance, but it is usually best not to combine one herb with another before you are actually ready to use the mixture. The one exception is *bouquet garni*, which can be prepared as for freezing—i.e. made up and tied with twists of cotton—and kept in a screwtop jar. Do not worry too much about little muslin sachets for the *bouquets*; by the time you use them you will be so accustomed to the flavour of herbs that you will not mind if some of the mixture falls into the casserole!

6 ～ Recipes

There are so many very good cookery books which list herbs among the ingredients that only a few recipes are included here; however, they are chosen to complement the basic garden of thirty plants.

Note: The recipes are to serve four.

ANGELICA

Candied Angelica

This recipe can be used for candying flowers.

a handful of young healthy angelica stems
1.4 litres (2½ pints) water
a handful of cooking salt
675 g (1½ lb) castor or granulated sugar

Cut the stems into suitable lengths of about 75 mm (3 in). Place them in a heatproof basin, boil 570 ml (1 pint) of water with the salt, pour it over the stems and leave for 24 hours. Drain the liquid off the stems and peel the outer pith from them. Place 850 ml (1½ pints) of water in a saucepan and dissolve the sugar in it slowly, then increase the heat and boil the sugar and water together for 10 minutes until they have formed a light syrup. Add the peeled angelica stems and continue to boil for another 20 minutes. Take a large wire or nylon mesh colander and drain the angelica, retaining the syrup. Leave the stems on the strainer for 3 days, covering them with sealing wrap.

After the 3 days boil again, using the same syrup mixture. This time leave the stems to cool in the liquid in the pan, then repeat the draining process for another 3 days. By now the stems will have stiffened and will be saturated with the sugar syrup. Sprinkle more castor sugar over them and bottle them in screwtop jars.

BALM

Duck stuffing

1 onion
1 large cooking apple
a handful of lemon balm leaves
a pinch of salt

Dice the onion and apple finely and mix with the salt and balm leaves. Score the inside of the duck with a sharp knife and fill the cavity with the stuffing, rubbing it into the score-marks. Cook the duck normally; the fatty taste will be cut and the flavour of apples and lemon balm will seep into the meat.

BASIL

Ricotta omelette

Omelette:
  8 eggs
  3 tablespoons butter
Filling and dressing:
  1 coffee-cup olive oil
  1 small chopped onion
  225 g (8 oz) Ricotta cheese
  2 sprigs chopped basil
  a sprig of parsley, chopped
  4 tomatoes, chopped and seeded
  a pinch of salt, pepper
  3 rounded tablespoons grated Parmesan cheese

Make the dressing by heating the oil and adding the onion, salt, diced tomatoes and basil. Cook gently for 15 minutes. Meanwhile, beat the Ricotta with 2 tablespoons of the Parmesan, the salt and a little parsley until you have a lightly whipped mixture. Beat the eggs with the rest of the grated Parmesan and a little salt and pepper.

    Heat a serving dish and keep it in a warm oven while you use half the egg mixture to make a flat omelette in a heavy frying pan. Pour the Ricotta filling onto the omelette and place it in the oven while you hastily make a second omelette from the remaining egg mixture, and place it over the first omelette, rather like making a layer cake. Cover the omelette with the oily tomato sauce. Serve while still hot and cut into four.

Genoese pesto or green herb sauce

Pine nuts can be bought from many delicatessens in Britain, especially from Cypriot or Greek shops. Parmesan cheese is suggested here, but if you can obtain Pecorino from an Italian supplier, use that.

2 bunches basil leaves
1 dessertspoon chopped pine nuts (or blanched walnuts)
6 cloves of garlic
2 sprigs marjoram
85 g (3 oz) Parmesan cheese (grated)
1 cup olive oil
2 tablespoons boiling water

Chop the herbs finely. Pound the herbs, nuts and crushed garlic in a mortar, or make them into a purée in a blender (moistening the ingredients with hot water if necessary). Add the cheese slowly, still mixing. Add the olive oil a little at a time, making sure each addition is blended in before adding more. Finally, add the hot water to thin the pesto to suit your own taste. It is delicious simply spread on bread, although it is intended to pour over pasta, in which case it will be necessary to heat it very slowly. Do not allow pesto to boil.

BAY

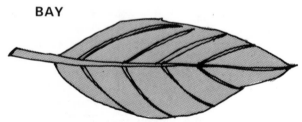

Boudin de Volaille

This white sausage is traditionally served in France on Christmas Eve. Many butchers will be pleased to sell you sausage skins so that you can make your own. It's also a good way to use up leftovers.

450 g (1 lb) minced white chicken meat, including as much breast as possible
225 g (8 oz) fat bacon, minced
4 egg whites
2 tablespoons finely chopped onion
2 cups cold boiled milk

knob of butter
1 bay leaf
thyme to taste
nutmeg
salt and pepper
sausage skins

Mix the chicken and bacon. Fry the onions until soft and add them to the meat. Add the egg whites slowly, mixing them in as you do so; add all the seasonings and mix well. Strain any surplus liquid off the meat mixture, then add the milk, mix again and remove the bay leaf. Fill the sausage skins. Poach the sausages in hot water for 10 minutes, then prick and fry or grill them until they are golden brown.

Aigo-Sau

A bay leaf is the staple of every bouquet garni, *the mixture of herbs used to season nearly all casseroles and marinades. Here it is used with fish and in a bouquet more suitable for a version of the Provençal bouillabaisse than the rosemary, thyme, parsley and bay version. This is a quickly made dish.*

450 g (1 lb) white fish
1 onion, finely chopped
3 waxy potatoes
3 cloves of garlic
2 large tomatoes, chopped and seeded
salt, pepper
6 slices thickly cut white bread
bouquet garni: 1 large bay leaf, sprigs of fennel, thyme, parsley and celery leaf
1 tablespoon oil

Clean the fish and use heads to add flavour. To keep the flavour correct you may add heads discarded by the fishmonger. Put the fish in a large stewing pot with the tomatoes, onion, garlic and herbs as well as the peeled, sliced potatoes. Add salt and pepper and sprinkle on the oil. Mix all the ingredients and add just enough water to cover them. Bring to the boil and cook at simmering point until the potatoes are cooked. Remove the fish heads and serve the stew on slices of bread. The liquid is traditionally served as soup, followed by the fish as a main course.

BERGAMOT

Bergamot tea

Use an enamel or stainless steel pan.

Allow 1 teaspoon of bergamot leaves per person, add to them as many cups of water as are necessary and simmer for 10 minutes. Strain off the tea and add sugar or honey to sweeten.

Bergamot milk is refreshing at bedtime and induces sleep; allow 1 tablespoon dried bergamot leaves to 285 ml ($\frac{1}{2}$ pint) milk and simmer for 5 minutes before straining.

BORAGE

Borage can be made into tea in a similar way. However, its chief use is as an addition to summer drinks.

BURNET

Burnet vinegar

Lightly fill a jar or wide-mouthed bottle with burnet leaves.

Add enough vinegar to cover the leaves and leave for 2 weeks. Use the cucumber-flavoured vinegar for salad dressings.

Burnet leaves are also delicious with cream cheese in sandwiches, or sprinkled over salads.

CHERVIL

Commonly used in French recipes, often in place of parsley. Chervil should not be cooked too long.

Chervil soup

6 tablespoons chopped fresh chervil leaves
1.1 litres (2 pints) hot stock, preferably chicken or vegetable
3–4 rounded tablespoons flour
55 g (2 oz) butter
A little single cream and some extra chervil leaves for garnish

Melt the butter in a heavy pan and gently stew the chervil leaves in it. Add the flour and mix well into the leaves, stir until a *roux* has formed. Add a little stock and stir until the mixture thickens and makes a sauce. Add the rest of the stock slowly, stirring all the time. Simmer for 20 minutes, serve with a little cream and chopped leaves.

Le farçon (mashed potatoes from the Savoy district)

1.4 kg (3 lb) potatoes
1½ tablespoons castor sugar
6 eggs
285 ml (½ pint) milk
1 tablespoon chopped chervil, or more if wished
nutmeg
salt, pepper

Boil the potatoes in their skins, peel them while they are still warm and mash them. If necessary, blend to get a rich thick purée, and combine this with the salt, pepper, sugar and a sprinkling of nutmeg, all folded well in. Beat the eggs and heat the milk, add both to the mashed potatoes

with the chervil, and mix the ingredients again. Butter the base of a wide shallow ovenproof dish and fill it with the potato mixture. Brown in a very hot oven for 10 minutes.

CHIVES

Chive butter

For a snack on toast or as a savoury mix, mix 3 tablespoons of chopped chives with 55–85 g (2–3 oz) warm butter. It's delicious spread thickly on hot toast.

Rabbit and mushroom casserole with chives

In Normandy large field mushrooms called 'pieds de mouton', or sheeps' feet, are used in this recipe. Field mushrooms have more flavour, if you can find them.

1 rabbit, cut into pieces
225 g (8 oz) mushrooms
115 g (4 oz) butter
3 onions, sliced
6 juniper berries, crushed
1 clove of garlic, crushed
bouquet garni
285 ml (½ pint) mild beer
1 tablespoon vinegar
1 tablespoon French mustard
2 tablespoons chopped chives
salt, pepper

Cut the mushrooms into big pieces if they are very large, otherwise use them whole. Add a few drops of the vinegar to a cup of boiling water, place the mushrooms in a colander, and scald them with the water and vinegar. Melt the butter in a heavy iron casserole and fry the rabbit in it until it is golden brown, turning it regularly to avoid sticking. Add the onions and continue cooking until they are soft. Add the salt, pepper, crushed juniper berries, crushed garlic and the *bouquet garni*, then the beer except for one tablespoon, and the rest of the vinegar.

Combine the ingredients and keep the casserole on a high heat for about 15 minutes so that the beer reaches boiling point and reduces slightly. Add the mushrooms, mixing them into the meat, and simmer on a low heat for 1 hour. Remove the *bouquet garni*, mix the mustard with the remaining beer and add it. Stir in the chives and serve at once.

COMFREY

For some suggestions on the use of comfrey in the kitchen, see p. 32.

DILL

Dill seed bread

340 g (12 oz) white flour
225 g (8 oz) cottage cheese
1 sachet dry yeast
9 teaspoons sugar
2 teaspoons dill seeds
2 tablespoons warm water
2 tablespoons shredded onion
2 eggs
40 g (1½ oz) butter
sea salt
a pinch of baking powder

In a small bowl mix the warm water, yeast and 1 teaspoon sugar and leave for 5 minutes. Mix again and leave for 10 minutes in a warm place until the yeast works and the mixture bubbles and swells up. In a small pan, melt 30 g (1 oz) of the butter, add the onions and cook until glassy but not brown. Mix together the flour, the rest of the sugar, the salt and baking powder in a large mixing bowl, and make a well in the centre. Gradually stirring in the flour, add the onions and butter, the yeast mixture, the cheese, 1 egg and the dill seed. Stir until you have a ball of dough detaching from the sides of the bowl.

Knead the dough on a wooden board or marble slab, sprinkling on enough flour to make a firm elastic mixture. Return the dough to the bowl, melt the rest of the butter and smooth it over the surface of the ball of dough. Cover the bowl with a clean cloth and place it in a warm place to prove for at least 1 hour or until the dough has doubled in size. Grease a 225×125 mm (9×5 in) loaf tin, place the dough in the tin and leave for another ½ hour in a warm place.

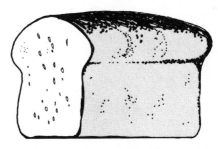

Preheat the oven to 375°F (Regulo 5–6). Brush the top of the loaf with the other egg beaten in milk and bake for 30 minutes. Test by rapping the base of the loaf when it is removed from the tin; if it sounds hollow it is done. If it does not, bake for another 5–10 minutes. Turn onto a wire rack to cool; if wished, paint the surface with softened butter and coarse sea salt.

Gravad lax

Dill can be tasted at its best in this recipe, which is almost the national dish of Scandinavian countries. Although expensive, it makes a treat when salmon is cheapest. Alternatively, use frozen salmon. The dish is served as a first course, when this amount will satisfy six people. The leaves of dill are usually called 'weed'.

680 g (1 lb 8 oz) tail of salmon
2 large tablespoons fresh dill leaves
1 tablespoon sea salt
1 teaspoon crushed black peppercorns or coarsely ground pepper
2 tablespoons castor sugar
1 tablespoon brandy (if possible)
1 egg yolk
2 tablespoons French mustard
1 cup olive oil
2 tablespoons wine vinegar
salt, pepper

Skin the fish and fillet it into two pieces. Mix the sea salt, half the sugar and dill, the brandy and peppercorns into a pickle mixture. Spread a quarter of the pickle mix on the bottom of a dish and lay one piece of salmon over it. Add another quarter of pickle mix over the salmon, then add the rest of the fish and finally cover it with the rest of the mixture, rubbing it into the fish. Cover the salmon with silver foil and a heavy board with a weight on top of it, and leave in a cool place, or in a refrigerator if closely covered, for at least 2 days, turning the salmon in the pickle every day. It will keep up to 5 days in a refrigerator. The compressed salmon can be sliced downwards when it is served. A sauce is made from the mustard beaten with the remaining sugar and an egg yolk to which the oil and vinegar are added slowly, continually beating as with a mayonnaise. Add the remaining dill, salt and pepper to the sauce.

FENNEL

Stuffed fish

Any white fish, cleaned and gutted but whole

6 slices white bread in crumbs
milk
1 handful chopped fennel
other herbs to taste: parsley, chervil, tarragon
butter
salt and pepper

Soak the breadcrumbs in milk and add the herbs, including the chopped fennel leaves. Stuff the fish with the breadcrumb mixture and lay it in a greased baking dish. Rub the butter over the fish skin and cook for at least 20 minutes, depending on the size of the fish, at 375°F (Regulo 5–6).

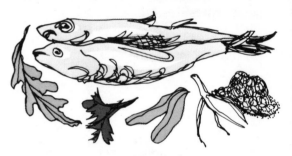

Florence fennel au gratin

This is the root which looks like a compact celery and which is worth cultivating in rows in the vegetable garden as a salad ingredient as well as a braising vegetable.

1 large fennel root
55 g (2 oz) Parmesan cheese
55 g (2 oz) breadcrumbs
butter

Chop the fennel root into several large pieces and cook them for 20 minutes in boiling water. When it is tender, remove and drain the fennel and put it in a greased fireproof dish. Sprinkle with the cheese and breadcrumbs mixed together and a few dabs of butter. Place in a very hot oven until the cheese melts and becomes golden.

GERANIUM

Rose-scented geranium cream

3 rose-scented geranium leaves
285 ml ($\frac{1}{2}$ pint) double cream
170 g (6 oz) cream cheese
55 g (2 oz) castor sugar

Using a double boiler pan, if possible, heat
the cream over hot water, stirring in the
sugar and geranium leaves. When the cream
is hot but before it boils, remove from the
heat and allow it to cool. Place the cream
cheese in a dish and blend in the cream,
including the leaves. Cover and leave in the
refrigerator overnight. Before serving the
cream, take out the leaves, or remove them
whilst eating.

HORSERADISH

Sauce for trout

1 horseradish root, grated
1 small carton (140 ml, 5 fl oz) sour cream
55 g (2 oz) walnuts
1 teaspoon herb mustard or French
    mustard

Pour boiling water over the shelled walnuts
and when cool peel off the fine brown
skin. Chop the nuts into small pieces and
mix with the sour cream, mustard and
grated horseradish. Serve with trout or
beef.

HYSSOP

Hyssop is not much used in British cooking, though it is still added to salads in the
South of France, and to fruit cups and pies
in the United States.

JUNIPER

*Juniper appears with nearly all strong-
tasting game either in the marinade or in
the recipe. In Germany it is sometimes
added to sauerkraut.*

Jugged hare, German style

1 hare, cut into pieces
225 g (8 oz) streaky bacon
3 onions, sliced
4 slices rye bread in crumbs
3 cloves garlic (including 1 crushed clove)
1 bay leaf
6 juniper berries, crushed
1 bottle red wine
1 cup stock
salt, pepper, nutmeg

Place the hare, breadcrumbs, onions and diced bacon in a heavy casserole in layers, adding, as you arrange them, all the seasonings. Add the stock and the wine. Cover closely and cook in a slow oven for 1½–2 hours or until the hare is tender.

LAVENDER

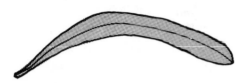

Lavender sugar was once sprinkled on pies and cakes and it is quite simple to make, but perhaps a small screwtop jarful would suffice as it is really only a novelty.

Crush some lavender heads and mix them with an equal quantity of castor sugar. Leave them for a few weeks so that the oil can permeate the sugar, then sieve off the sugar and use it.

LOVAGE

Lentil hors-d'œuvre

225 g (8 oz) lentils
olive oil
2 hard-boiled eggs
chopped spring onions or thin rounds of
    red onions, raw, to taste
a handful of fresh lovage leaves

Soak the lentils overnight, then cook them in water for 1 hour. Drain them, add the olive oil and onion, and place in a serving dish. Slice the hard-boiled eggs and arrange on top of the lentils, with plenty of lovage as a garnish.

MARJORAM

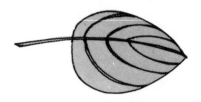

Italian lamb with white wine

1 kilo (2 lb 3 oz) leg of lamb
½ orange
2 carrots
2 tomatoes
2 sticks celery
2 onions
1 glass white wine
2–3 cloves of garlic, crushed
1 tablespoon chopped marjoram
2 tablespoons oil
salt and pepper

Heat the oil in a heavy pan or iron casserole and fry the sliced onions until soft. Mix the crushed garlic, marjoram leaves, salt and pepper, and rub it over the meat. Place the lamb in the pan and brown it on all sides, and add the chopped tomatoes, carrots and celery. Cook on a fairly high heat for 10 minutes. Add the white wine, return to boiling point and cook on high heat for 2 minutes. Reduce to simmering heat, cover the pan and cook for 2 hours. Before bringing the meat to the table add the juice of the ½ orange, squeezing it over the meat.

Oregano and tomato sauce for grilled meat

1 tablespoon chopped oregano or 1½ table-
    spoons marjoram
3 tablespoons oil
3 cloves of garlic, crushed
450 g (1 lb) ripe tomatoes

Scald the tomatoes and peel them, slice them into quarters and remove the seeds. Heat the oil and fry the garlic until it smokes, add the tomatoes and chopped herbs, reducing the heat, sprinkle with salt and pepper and allow the tomatoes to cook to a thick purée. If wished, lightly grill the meat, then finish it in the pan with the sauce.

Without peeling or coring the apples, cut them into pieces. Add the vinegar to 570 ml (1 pint) of water and pour over the apples in a pan. Add the mint and stir. Simmer until the apples are soft, then strain the liquid through a jelly bag. Add 450 g (1 lb) sugar for every pint of liquid. Return the liquid to a pan and dissolve the sugar in it. Boil hard to setting point. Before bottling, add a few fresh mint leaves and a few drops of green colouring to the jelly. When the liquid is cool skim off the foam, and stir once more before pouring into wide-mouthed jars which have been heated. Leave to finish setting in the jars. Serve with lamb.

MINTS

Orange mint sauce
(to accompany lamb)

140 ml (¼ pint) orange juice
140 ml (¼ pint) lemon juice
2 rounds fresh pineapple, shredded
1 tablespoon finely chopped mint leaves
sugar to taste

Mix all ingredients together and leave in a warm place for 2 hours before using.

Bottled mint jelly

450 g (1 lb) cooking apples
140 ml (¼ pt) wine vinegar
a handful of mint leaves
sugar
commercial green colouring

Yoghurt chilled soup (serves 6)

400 ml (14 fluid oz) natural yoghurt
1 large or 2 small cucumbers
a handful of fresh mint leaves
4 cloves of garlic, crushed

Place all the yoghurt except 1 tablespoon-ful in a large jug or bowl which fits in the refrigerator. Crush the peeled garlic to a paste and add the remaining yoghurt to it, stir, and add the mixture to the jug or bowl of yoghurt. Peel the cucumber and grate it into the yoghurt. Finely chop the mint leaves or put them through a Parslimint grinder, and add them to the soup. Stir, cover the jug or bowl and leave in the refrigerator for 2 hours before serving. Garnish with whole mint leaves.

PARSLEY

Persillade: *a mixture of finely chopped parsley with chopped shallot or garlic which is added to many meat and vegetable dishes just before they are served.*

Aubergines with persillade

2 aubergines
3 tablespoons oil
3 cloves of garlic, crushed
a handful of parsley
basil, thyme or marjoram may be added
    with the parsley

Cut the aubergines into thin rounds and place them in a colander with plenty of salt sprinkled over them, to drain off the liquid. Leave for 1 hour, then wipe the slices with a paper towel until they are dry. Warm the oil in a heavy pan and cook the aubergines on a low heat, turning them once. When they are soft and cooked remove them, drain them on paper towels and place them in a

dish in a warm oven. Increase the heat of the oil remaining in the pan and fry the parsley, herbs and garlic in it for an instant; as soon as the mixture starts to frizzle, remove it from the heat and pour it over the aubergines.

Fish cakes

225 g (8 oz) cooked, boned white fish
30 g (1 oz) butter
1 slice white bread
1 egg
milk
1 tablespoon finely chopped parsley
nutmeg, salt, pepper
oil

Flake the fish. Crumble the bread in the milk, then combine the fish and soaked breadcrumbs. Add the beaten egg, butter and parsley to form a firm paste. Season with salt, pepper and nutmeg and mould into round flat cakes. Heat the oil and fry the fish cakes.

PENNYROYAL

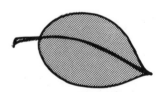

Pennyroyal is too pungent to be very useful in the kitchen, but used sparingly it can be employed to flavour peas or potatoes.

ROSEMARY

Use this herb to flavour vinegar and oil by steeping twigs in the liquid.

Roast lamb and bakehouse potatoes

Lamb joint
2 cloves garlic
1 kilo (2 lb 3 oz) potatoes
3 sprigs rosemary
coarse ground black pepper
butter (oil if desired)
salt

Slit the skin of the lamb and insert garlic slivers into it. Rub the joint with oil or butter and put it into the oven, preheated to 425°F (Regulo 7). When the lamb has been in the oven for 30 minutes, add the peeled and quartered potatoes which have been boiled for 10 minutes in salted water. Sprinkle salt, pepper, sprigs of rosemary and oil or knobs of butter on them before arranging them round the lamb. Cook them with the meat, turning them once to ensure both sides are brown and basting them with the butter and meat juices. To work out the total cooking time of lamb at this temperature, allow 20 minutes per lb plus 20 minutes extra.

SAGE

Sage and onion sauce

2 large onions, sliced
30 g (1 oz) butter
425 ml ($\frac{3}{4}$ pint) meat or chicken stock
55 g (2 oz) white breadcrumbs
1 dessertspoon chopped sage leaves
salt, pepper

Brown the onions in the butter, add the stock and breadcrumbs, stir until the sauce thickens, then add the sage, salt and pepper.

Stuffed cucumbers

Use ridge cucumbers, which are much easier to grow than the usual type and which have a sweet strong flavour.

4 small ridge cucumbers
4 sage leaves
1 large onion
30 g (1 oz) fresh breadcrumbs
milk
15 g ($\frac{1}{2}$ oz) butter

Cut a lid off the end of each cucumber and scoop out the pips with an apple corer. Turn onto a flat end and allow the cucumber to drain. Chop the onion and *sauté* it in the butter until soft, then mix it with the finely chopped sage. Soak the breadcrumbs in as much milk as they will absorb and mix with the onions and sage. Sprinkle salt and pepper into the cucumbers and stuff them with the mixture, using a teaspoon. Replace the end pieces and bake at 300°F (Regulo 2) for 45 minutes.

SAVORY

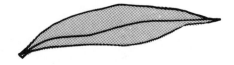

Broad beans in the French manner

1 kilo (2 lb 3 oz) fresh broad beans
55 g (2 oz) butter
1 teaspoon sugar
2 sprigs savory
small carton (140 ml, 5 fl oz) double cream
1 egg yolk
salt, pepper

Shell the beans and cook them in boiling salted water for 10 minutes. In another pan, melt the butter, then add the drained beans with the sugar, savory and seasoning. Cover the pan and allow the beans to stew gently in the butter for 20 minutes, shaking them occasionally. Meanwhile, beat the egg yolk into the cream. When the beans are cooked, remove the pan from the heat and stir in the egg yolk and cream. Serve at once.

SORREL

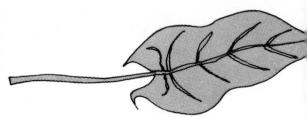

Note: Sorrel should not be eaten by sufferers from kidney trouble.

Simple sorrel purée

680 g (1½ lb) sorrel
55 g (2 oz) butter
salt

Wash the young leaves several times, prepare a pan of boiling water and blanch the sorrel leaves in it for 2 minutes. Drain them. Melt the butter in a heavy pan and add the sorrel and a sprinkling of salt. Stir until cooked. Liquidise if you wish.

SWEET CICELY

Can be used as a sweetener to reduce the amount of sugar needed in recipes. See p. 48.

TARRAGON

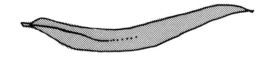

The classic tarragon and chicken dish is simply to fill the cavity of a roasting fowl with tarragon sprigs and roast it on a high heat, basting the fowl with butter. Alternatively, the cavity can be flavoured with a knob of softened butter mixed with tarragon leaves.

Fricassée of chicken with tarragon and cream sauce

1 fresh chicken, cut into four
55 g (2 oz) butter
140 ml ($\frac{1}{4}$ pint) chicken stock (made from a cube)
1 glass white wine
1 small carton (140 ml, 5 fl oz) single cream
3 sprigs fresh tarragon plus 1 tablespoon finely chopped tarragon leaves
salt, black pepper, cayenne pepper

Using a large heavy-based pan, melt the butter and gently brown the chicken pieces in it. Add the sprigs of tarragon and the seasonings. By now the meat will have exuded enough juice to form a brown glaze on the base on the pan; add the wine and deglaze the juices with a wooden spoon so that a thick liquid is formed. Add the stock and turn the chicken over in the liquid until it is cooked, in about 20 minutes. Remove the chicken pieces and keep them warm while you add the cream to the pan, lowering the heat. Stir until the sauce drops slowly from the spoon. Strain this sauce over the chicken pieces and sprinkle with the finely chopped pieces of tarragon leaf.

Mushrooms with thyme

450 g (1 lb) button mushrooms
3 tablespoons olive oil
thyme to taste

This recipe is for lovers of thyme, so the quantity depends on your own taste. Wash the mushrooms and cut off any dirty stems. Heat the oil in a heavy pan, and when it is smoking put in the mushrooms and cover the pan, allowing the mushrooms to stew for 8–10 minutes; they will produce plenty of juice so the pan will not burn. Remove the lid and add a pinch of salt and the thyme, detaching the leaves from the stalks. Cook at a high temperature with the lid removed until the water evaporates enough to leave a moist sauce of olive oil. Serve hot or cold.

THYME

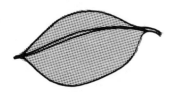

VERBENA

Verbena is not normally used in cooking—for some alternative ideas, see p. 50.

7 ~ Fragrant Herbs

Pot Pourris

One of the problems in making pot pourris is the necessity of fixatives which will keep the smells lasting. Londoners will find that Culpeper, 21 Bruton St. W1, not only stock the ingredients necessary for making pot pourri, but are also very helpful with advice and suggestions of added fragrances which can be bought in the shop and combined with those scented flowers and herbs you have culled from the garden. Culpeper have several branches in other towns too.

The usual fixatives are orris root, gum benzoin and rose oil. If you intend to make a lot of pot pourris and give them as gifts, it's as well to invest in these. However, perfectly good pot pourris, lasting several months, can be made without any fixatives, and if you are experimenting with herbs and their uses it might be better to start off with some of these, and graduate to more long-lasting mixtures later on.

Incidentally, orris root can be made at home after you have invested in the orris iris, which can be bought from specialist growers. The Latin name is *Iris Germanica* and as it was once the humble old-fashioned cottage iris it also might be possible to ask your local market garden or nurseryman about it. Obviously you will have to wait until side rhizomes have been formed before you expend them in pot pourri, but if you are a dedicated herb lover and if your garden is planted with a view to a long and useful future, it would be a good idea to plant some roots for orris in years to come. Once you are able to harvest spare rhizomes you will find that powdered orris is easy to make. Dry the root as if it were horseradish and then grate it or pulverise it in a blender. It won't smell until it is dried and powdered, so don't be disappointed when the root is first raised.

Dry the herbs separately and mix them afterwards. An all-herb mixture is composed of angelica, basil, bay leaves, bergamot, borage, lemon balm, lemon thyme, lemon verbena (dried lemon or orange peel can be used instead of this fragrance), lovage, marjoram, mints, rosemary, sage, scented-leaved geraniums, Sweet Cicely and tarragon. Any of these can be left out. You may either make up an all-herb mixture or combine it with flowers and spices. Practice will dictate your own favourites for the future, but meanwhile try out everything, making up different blends rather like a teablender and sniffing them over the next few months to see which you prefer. Place a small list in each dry mixture to remind you what the composition is, otherwise you will be hopelessly muddled.

Flower mixtures would include lavender, rose petals (preferably red), violets, jasmine, marigold petals, nasturtiums, camomile and, if possible, lime. Flowers with ephemeral fragrances like tobacco flowers and night scented stocks will not be suitable.

To either mixture, or a compound of herbs and flowers, can be added spices; these provide the bass notes in your musical composition so it's always a good idea to add some, though you must make sure that the richer smell does not predominate over the lighter flower fragrances. Use crushed cardomums, powdered cinnamon, whole cloves and grated nutmeg. Coriander and aniseed are also possible. If you can, crush or grind the spices just before using them, or ask the shop where you buy them to pulverise them in an electric blender. Many specialist health food stores will be pleased to do this for you.

When you have gathered the ingredients of the pot pourri in the morning of a warm dry day, pluck the petals and place them on flat newspaper in a dry dark place, turning them daily until they are dry and brittle. Then place them in large bowls, alternating the layers of herbs and flowers with spices. Finally, add the fixative, mixing the pot pourri as if you were blending ingredients in a cake to ensure that the fixative permeates the complete mixture. The top layer of your pot pourri should be the most decorative, perhaps with whole flower heads or using those petals which retain colour best such as roses, honeysuckle or violas. Cover the bowl with a close-fitting lid or sealing wrap and keep it in a dry dark place until you wish to use it.

When the summer is past and you want to remind yourself of its scents by perfuming the house with them, put the pot pourri in jars or bowls throughout the house. Occasionally turn the dried leaves so that the petals below will rise to the surface.

Lavender Pot Pourri

This demands a great deal of lavender, but it is extremely long-lasting. Until this century lavender was the most familiar country fragrance used in muslin sachets to scent sheets and handkerchiefs. Even today linen closets in old houses are still faintly perfumed with it, so it is no surprise that dried lavender will last for years. Strip the lavender heads early on a dry morning and leave the spikes spread on newspaper in the sun until the tiny flowerets leave the spikes easily. You will need at least 110 g (4 oz) to make the process worthwhile, but be warned—lavender weighs very little! Place it in bowls in living-rooms and bedrooms, or use it to make up sachets to put with underwear and bedlinen.

Rose Pot Pourri

This is the best and most long-lasting form of pot pourri, but it entails some expense in buying the essential oils and orris root. However, the fixative mixture will last for years and new flowers can be placed with the old ones to make another year's supply of pot pourri. The quantities seem large, but it will make a great deal of very good pot pourri which can be given away as Christmas presents as well as used in your own home. Unless you have a good supply of red roses it is almost impossible to make; for some reason red makes the strongest perfume in roses, as does white in other flowers.

Ingredients

50 heads of red roses
110 g (4 oz) powdered orris root
15 g ($\frac{1}{2}$ oz) oil of geranium
15 g ($\frac{1}{2}$ oz) oil of lavender
Spices: 25 g (1 oz) ground coriander, 25 g (1 oz) ground nutmeg, 25 g (1 oz) whole cloves, 3 sticks cinnamon, flaked
2 cups herb or flower pot pourri
salt

You will need sheets of newspaper and a large earthenware jar with a close-fitting lid—an old-fashioned bread crock or a large French casserole is ideal.

Pluck the rose petals early on a dry day and spread them on a newspaper in a dry, well-ventilated place. Turn them over daily until they are brittle and thin like old paper. Weigh the petals and take about three-quarters of their weight in kitchen salt. Mix it with the rose petals in the jar, and stir daily for a week. Add the other pot pourri—this can be a herb or flower mixture, using one of the previous recipes.

Use a very large mixing bowl or, if you have it, one of the traditional large pot-pourri bowls. Place the orris and some of the oils at the bottom and add the rest of the pot pourri, pouring in the remaining oils and spices, and mixing all the ingredients together very well, as if making a fruit cake.

Leave in a cool dark place for three to four weeks, then distribute in bowls or sachets.

Salt will moisten a pot pourri which becomes too dry, which often happens in houses where there is central heating. Alternatively, if the pot pourri becomes damp, a little extra orris can be added. In either case, stir the mixture with your fingers, not only to release the scents but also to ensure that the even consistency is retained. Pot pourri which dries too much may lose its fragrance and a damp mixture can become mouldy.

Herb Pillows

Recently there has been an interest in sleep-inducing herb pillows. They make very attractive presents, but they can be rather expensive to buy. Like cushions, they need an inner cover on which a loose cover is placed. The outer slip cover can be made of sprigged fine lawn, and in the summer sales small quantities can often be bought cheaply. Do not buy a fabric which is too heavy or the smell won't permeate it; Dacron is most suitable, or material like Liberty Tana Lawn.

Although it is possible to make tiny pads, anything smaller than 200 mm (8 in) square is not very practical. The simplest basic herb mixture is made of dried leaves of angelica, lavender, lemon verbena and peppermint-scented mint. Extra sleep-inducing herbs are dill, bergamot, lemon balm, marjoram, and sage or thyme. Hops can also be added; they can be bought from health food shops or from chemists who sell wine-making ingredients. Extra herbs could be rosemary, rosemary flowers and rose geranium petals.

If you make sachets to place among clothes, add southernwood to the herbs to deter moths. Extremely flat cushions or pads can be made to fill the bases of drawers, suitcases or linen chests.

Herb Oil

Herb oil is not only useful in cooking, it can be added to face creams to give them a herbal fragrance. Lavender is the most popular for cosmetics.

Herbs suitable for cooking oils are basil, thyme and tarragon. Crush the leaves by hand or in a blender, then add them to a bottle or jar of nut, maize, cornflower or olive oil in the proportion of 2 tablespoons of herb purée per half-pint of oil. Leave 12 mm ($\frac{1}{2}$ in) space at the top of the bottle and fill it up with wine vinegar. Leave the bottle or jar in full sunlight for several weeks, shaking it occasionally. Then strain off the oil, and repeat the process with a new ration of herbs and the original oil. By the end of the summer you will have a strong-smelling rich herbal mixture to add to salad dressings or to incorporate in special casserole dishes.

Metrication

LENGTH

mm	in		m	ft	in
12	0.5		1	3	3
25	1.0		2	6	7
75	3.0		3	9	11
100	3.9		4	13	1
200	7.9		5	16	5
300	11.8		6	19	8
400	15.7		7	22	11
500	19.7		8	26	3
600	23.6		9	29	6
700	27.6		10	32	8
800	31.5				
900	35.4				
1000	39.4				

1000 millimetres (mm)=1 metre (m)

WEIGHT

g	oz		kg	lb	oz
25	0.9		1	2	3
50	1.8		2	4	7
75	2.6		3	6	10
100	3.5		4	8	13
200	7.1		5	11	0
300	10.6				
400	14.1				
500	17.6				

1000 grams (g)=1 kilogram (kg)

CAPACITY

ml	fl oz		l	pts
50	1.8		1	1.7
100	3.5		1.2	2.1
150	5.3		1.4	2.5
200	7.0		1.6	2.8
300	10.6		1.8	3.2
400	14.1		2.0	3.5
500	17.6		3.0	5.3
600	21.1		4.0	7.0
			5.0	8.1

20 fluid oz=1 pint

1000 millilitres (ml)=1 litre (l)

OVEN TEMPERATURES

			Gas Regulo
Very cool	250°F	(121°C)	$\frac{1}{4}$
	275°F	(135°C)	$\frac{1}{2}$
Cool	300°F	(149°C)	1, 2
Warm	325°F	(163°C)	3
Moderate	350°F	(177°C)	4
Fairly hot	375°F	(191°C)	5
	400°F	(204°C)	6
Hot	425°F	(218°C)	7
Very hot	450°F	(232°C)	8
	475°F	(246°C)	9